Becoming
a
Superstar
Seller

Becoming
A
Superstar
Seller

Don Sheehan
with John O'Toole

amacom
AMERICAN MANAGEMENT ASSOCIATION

Library of Congress Cataloging in Publication Data

Sheehan, Don.
  Becoming a superstar seller.

  Includes index.
  1. Selling. I. O'Toole, John E.
II. Title.
HF5438.25.S476   1985
658.8′5   84-45820
ISBN 0-8144-5812-2

Printing number

10 9 8 7 6 5 4 3 2 1

Dedication

This book is fondly dedicated to all the men and women whose skill and determination have moved the lion's share of the world's goods and services into the right hands. By so doing they have enriched their own lives and the lives of those they serve. They deservedly wear the laurel of the superstar.

Foreword

Becoming a superstar salesperson is easy if you know how. Don Sheehan tells you how in this book. Superstar salespeople of the past and present include Larry Wilson, Bob Conklin, and Wes Fesler. Don Sheehan trained all three of them, and thousands of others over the past 30 years.

A superstar salesman for Colgate-Palmolive and the Dale Carnegie courses, Don Sheehan has written two best-selling books, *The Price Book* and *Shut Up and Sell!*, which has now been published in English, Spanish, and Japanese. In this sales guide, he shares sales expertise from his four decades of selling and training others to be professional salespeople.

Whether you sell a product or a service, you'll learn the success secrets necessary to excel in sales. You'll be taught the essential traits and habits of top pros through the seasoned eyes and ears of the master salesman and sales trainer, Don Sheehan.

The proven techniques and shortcuts in the following chapters are a treasury for new or experienced salespeople. I would have paid any price to learn these methods when I started selling years ago.

This book will inspire and motivate you. But, more than that, Don Sheehan's stories have the power to change your life and help you move up in the sales world. I know, because his training changed my life.

Robert L. Montgomery
Author, speaker, trainer

Introduction

A lot of people work for peanuts, but I can show them how to work for coconuts—lots of them.

I've flown more than a million miles, visited Moscow, lived overseas for over two years, including a very cold winter in Korea. I've been to Jerusalem where the Lord walked and talked. I'm over 50 years old and I'm grateful for what I've seen. From my experiences I can show you how to multiply yourself, how to be more effective. In other words, how to be a superstar.

To be a superstar you will need to know about motivating employees, getting new customers, managing your business, hiring the right people, getting the right prices, and using advertising. You will also need to understand cash flow, sales closings, delegation, prospecting, handling change, sales technique, and the ups and downs of our national economy.

You must realize that America is prone to recessions. I've seen eight of them since 1947. Most people don't know how to handle them; yet we have a recession about every two or three years.

As we near the mid-1980s, we have 15 million unemployed in Europe and 10 million unemployed in the United States, all because of wrong thinking. People are not really motivated. Most of these people see their own situation as being helpless, like a man from a General Motors plant who said, "I made $35,000 last year working at $18 an hour, but now I have no job." After he lost his well-paying position, he did not seek out any other employment opportunities. Too often apathy reigns when action—lots of it—is needed.

Superstars have the motivation and the energy to over-come periods of slack economy. They just get busy finding new customers. Superstars also understand that the same motivation and energy is necessary to stay on top when the economy is strong. If you examine the accounts you have right now, you will find that about half of them are really not profitable. By the time you wrestle them to the ground and get your money, you wonder who won. There is no way you are going to win unless you can find 50 percent more customers.

Another way to stay ahead in a recession—though this is equally important when the economy is booming—is to keep an eagle eye on operating costs. Profit margins are the lowest since the Civil War. To increase yours you must learn to save on what you need to buy to do business. I saved my company $100,000 in two and a half years by calculating, knowing what our costs were, taking advan-tage of discounts, and making substitutions. You must challenge every price quoted, because every supplier has about five sets.

A lot of people think they have to cut prices during a recession to keep the customers coming in. Yet you really have to increase your prices. Because you make fewer sales in a recession, you have to earn more money per sale to cover overhead. I almost went out of business during the first recession I experienced because I didn't understand this simple idea.

Most of you may have to increase your prices as much as 20 percent just to survive, but, strangely enough, the higher your prices are, the more you'll sell—as I show in my book *The Price Book*.

One of the most critical areas to concentrate on during a recession is advertising. Did you know that 80 percent of all businesses that fail do so because they don't advertise properly? To stress the last point, let me ask you whether you have been thrilled with the business newspaper adver-tising has brought you in the last year. If your answer is no, I'm not surprised; that's what we've found all around the country. And for good reason: readership is down to only 15 to 18 percent of the population. Have you been buried in customers from your Yellow Pages, radio, or TV advertising? The answer again is probably no.

For the superstar seller, just a few things are pulling today; among them are direct mail and phone calls. In fact, mail is "hot." A letter-type promotional piece is hot, and the postcard is even hotter. The postcard is actually revolutionizing many businesses, both wholesale and retail. Whatever type of business you're in, you're going to find that sending postcards is one of the most effective things you can do.

The telephone is also exciting and could make some of you millionaires. It's a great way to cover a lot of territory and get a job done.

The main thing to remember about promotion is that you must do it 12 months out of the year if you hope to improve your cash flow. It may be tempting to try to economize if things are tight, but you won't get the results you're looking for unless your promotion is continuous.

Last year my sales training business increased its profits $800 a week—not bad for a company that has been around for 27 years. We did it because we were willing to try new approaches, and because we kept at it constantly.

Yet money alone won't do it. There is only one person in a company who builds sales: the seller. The more super the seller, the more super the cash flow.

★★★★★★★★ **Contents** ★★★★★★★★

Becoming
a
Superstar
Seller

★★★★★★★★★ **CHAPTER 1** ★★★★★★★★★

What Makes a Superstar Seller

What makes sellers into superstars? They are rare commodities, these few; they sit with the elite. They are really something special. They have other names: buck smellers, profit makers, high earners, high grossers, maximizers.

Minneapolis millionaire Frank Tussler, a favorite student of mine, once said, "Hell, I don't want just a good year, I want a great year!" This is exactly the attitude of superstars. They want it right now. They are members of the "Now Generation." They don't want to wake up when they're 40 years old and say, "Well, look at all the mistakes I've made; now why haven't I made any money?"

What Makes a Superstar?

Superstars are truly standouts among thousands. They sell three or four times more than the average seller. How do they do it? What makes them tick?

Here are some of the things we know about superstars.

1. They have learned to learn. If they don't know something, they don't stumble around like dancers with two left feet; they get busy and learn it. If they are slow learners, they never make excuses. They stay up at night to learn what they need to know to sell.

2. They do things that produce business. You don't see them on long coffee breaks or killing the time of day. If they make any killings, it's with their sales. They are all business.

3. They become experts in products, in techniques, in approaching a prospect, in closing sales. They practice; they rehearse.

4. They do good jobs in managing themselves. They do not complain that there's not enough time in the day; they use their time. They have good personal habits. They are usually well groomed, eat right, sleep right, and train for the job, just like Olympic athletes, because they are out for the selling Olympics. They are in bed at the right time. They are out of bed at the right time. They do more of the right things and look for better ways to do them.

5. They are strategists. They always have a game plan. "This is what I'm going to do to sell more homes this month, and this is what I'm going to do to get more business." They are always in the future, not crying about what happened in the past. They do not alibi. If they have a poor week or month, they don't make excuses. They get right in there and try to correct things next month.

6. They are innovators. They create instead of compete. They won't compete with anyone but themselves.

7. They are always improving themselves, constantly taking courses, reading books, buying tapes. Superstars are students to the end.

8. They know they are effective, on-the-ball people. They take real pride in being on time, in doing the job, and in keeping their promises. They are the competent ones of this generation.

9. They have goals. They know what they want to sell in the coming days, weeks, and even years. Their future plans give them the spark that ignites their rockets to stardom. This is what makes them diamond-studded, gold-plated sellers. Their dreams put them where the air is thin. There isn't much company up in their stratosphere, but they are not lonely. They are too busy succeeding.

10. They get along with people: their associates, their fellow employees. They are good at getting people to support their ideas. They don't turn other people off. If you're fighting with someone, how can you sell him your ideas?

Superstars treat their own staffs, dealers, service people—everybody who works with them—just like customers. They don't distinguish between staff and customers, because they know that if they can't sell their own people, they will be out of luck with their customers. Superstars are diplomats, politicians who get along with everyone.

11. They know their strengths and weaknesses, and work to enhance the former and eliminate the latter. They are too open-minded to say, "I have no weaknesses. Take a look at me. I'm the last perfect person created." Superstars recognize that they have problems, but they do something about them.

12. They are eager for the new. They look hard at what is different that will affect their business.

To sum it up, you might say that the superstar is a real professional while the dime-a-dozen seller is, for all practical purposes, just an amateur. And remember: "Professionals can do the job even when they do not feel like it. Amateurs can't even do it when they feel like it."

Some people resent superstars because they are aggressive, but superstars are not particularly interested in winning popularity contests. Their counterparts, supersloths, prefer the old glad hand from the gang. Superstars get the job done; run-of-the-mill salespeople just *hope* to get it done. The real difference between superstars and amateurs is that superstars get results while the good time Charlies are busy daydreaming.

Superstars are tough people. They know how to do an "inside job" on themselves, and they work hard at it. They are gutsy, daring, and imaginative. They can put deals together on top of deals. They want to do it, and they want to do it now. Talk to them about making big dollars two or three years from now, and they will look at you as if you're crazy. They will say, "How about right now, this month!" They are not excited about what you tell them will happen tomorrow. For superstars, tomorrow is just another today, which they will be ready, willing, and able to handle when it comes.

Special Traits of Superstars

If superstars seem, like cats, to have nine lives, it could be because they have a number of special traits.

1. They do things differently. Most people try to screen "different" sellers out of their business, but smart operators deliberately look for them.

2. Superstars are usually loners. They do not sit around drinking coffee and eating lunch with a bunch of idlers. That bores them. They do not need anyone to fill up vacuums in their lives.

3. They start early in life. They are usually making a buck by the time they are nine, or twelve at the latest. They learned through good parents, good teachers, or good friends—maybe all three—that success isn't a personal chauffeur, it won't wait until you are ready.

4. Superstars have strong self-control. Inwardly superstars may be angry at buyers yet still hold their tempers, at least enough to make the sale. Usually they are impatient with others, but they won't show it.

5. They are happiest when they are in charge, because

they are leaders. About the only thing they like to follow is a good lead on a sale.

6. They can talk. Eighty percent of the people in America who make over $50,000 are those who are good on their feet, who can speak in front of others. They can see opportunities. They like individual thinking, not group thinking.

7. They are something much rarer—and sometimes even better—than good talkers: good listeners. Real sellers even listen while they talk. They know enough to can the chatter long before their clients nod off. They will, as I've said so often, "shut up and sell."

8. Superstars put first things first. When they are working, they work. When they can loaf, they loaf. They know they have only one candle to burn and that they can find their way by lighting just one end.

9. It's an absolute must that they sell so they can live with themselves. They do not worry about being rolling stones. They don't want to gather moss, they want to sell it. They have the killer instinct when it comes to the close. They know why they are there.

Superstars are actors. They will put on a performance for the close. They rehearse their parts. They are politicians and will kiss babies. They will do anything, as long as it's legal, to make a sale. They try to keep emotions under control all the time because highs and lows wear them out. They can always be friendly and smile.

They do not assume anything. They have 100 percent concentration during the close. Their eyes are on the prospect, not on the furniture. They know the words to five or six different closes. (Most sellers know two, but habitually use one.) The mediocre seller doesn't understand the urgency of the close. The superstar closes today. Right now.

They can spot oral and physical buying signals. They can sell from the sales center or from the prospect's home. They will not ask people to sign contracts, but only to "okay agreements." When they ask a closing question, they shut up. To them this is the greatest rule in selling: The first person who talks, loses. They use restraint and discipline to stay in command. When they sense a close, they will spend a day if necessary to get it. They will skip lunch if they need the time. They would even skip rope if it made a sale.

They understand that 75 percent of all closings are made on the first interview, approximately 20 percent on the second, and 5 percent on the third. They realize that the big show is the first interview.

They are tough-minded and know that 75 percent of all American home sales are made in the seller's mind before they see a possible buyer. A mindless approach, they know, is worse than no contact at all. A superstar's eleventh commandment is, "If thou canst not make up thine own mind, thou sure as shootin' can't make up thy client's mind." They plan to use their second wind when the close comes, but they do not get windy. They expect a fight. They expect some resistance if they are going to get their price, but at that point they have enough skill and determination to finish the job.

Superstars are rising stars, not falling ones.

CHAPTER 2

Lighting
the Fire

What motivates superstars to be Number One in sales, to be in the spotlight, to be the first to sell new products, to collect the most cash, to become seller of the year? Praise by the boss, recognition in the company newsletter, bonuses, cash and merchandise prizes, trips, motivation tapes, sales meetings, titles such as "senior salesperson," outside seminars, and more responsibility will all fire superstars, but it is money that gets them to exploit their potential.

How Superstars Keep Going

Once superstars have been motivated, they use five kinds of fuel and lubricants to keep them going.

1. *Even if they sense they are failing, they keep their enthusiasm high enough to turn disaster into success.*
2. *They stay away from negative salespeople, and they also stay away from negative customers.*
3. *They invest 3 to 5 percent of their time in improving themselves with books, seminars, and tapes.*
4. *They are always trying to perfect their techniques. One seller spent $600 to fly from Atlantic City to Minneapolis just to learn more closing ideas.*
5. *They love people and work hard to make their selling help others.*

Superstars teach themselves to reject rejection. They look on a failure to sell as a way to learn something. Positive-thinking sellers count their blessings after turndowns. At least they had opportunities to test their techniques. Rejection is part of the game of life, but the great sellers continue to play the game with gusto.

The big secret of superstars is that they are the 5 percent who truly actualize themselves by making the 100 percent commitment needed to do their jobs. They are the nuggets among the pebbles in the prospector's pan.

The National Science Foundation made a 20-year study of 1,500 American families and found that, among the 1,083 families which continued to report their finances, 88 had an average net worth of $1.2 million after 20 years.

How did they become millionaires? Was it from diamonds, gold, silver, big insurance, inheritance, selling their businesses, or belonging to the country club? None of these. They became wealthy by taking the jobs they had and giving them everything they could every day. At first, some did not even like their jobs, but they became all fired up once they got going. They became absorbed in their tasks. They forgot the hours.

Supersellers are not frantic people. They just work at an even intensity every day. Life is a hard, do-it-yourself job, so you must push the positive when you speak, write, or think. Stay away from the negative people who make up 85-90 pecent of the population.

Work an extra one to three hours daily to reduce debts. Take "if" out of your life by adding "I will." Stay off the roller coaster of emotion. Strive for full days of intense work. People don't break down from outside, but from inside. Superstars produce daily. They are not all money hungry, but are balanced spiritually, socially, and economically. If you are going to stay a winner, you need a more spiritual attitude plus the self-control to curb your eating, drinking, and emotions.

Winning, not losing, is the philosophy of superstars. If you are a superstar, you should have as many winning characteristics as possible. You should smile more, be helpful to others, keep your ears open, ask questions rather than make statements.

As a superstar you will reflect optimism in your dress and your friendly, relaxed warmth. I don't think I've ever met a winner who wasn't humble enough to keep on learning. Winners have the courage to relax, to tell the truth, to develop new ideas, to be willing to give fair consideration to the opinions of others.

Losers have their own special qualities. If you have any loser traits, throw them out as fast as you can. They are your tenants, so treat them like any other nonpaying guests. Give them notice before they break you.

Losers are quick to haul out the crying towel. They like to criticize rather than look at the positive side. They are too narrow-minded to read anything or to correct their own bad habits. You can spot the targets for failure by their sloppy dress, their vulgar laughter, their inconsiderateness. Generally, you will find a loser doing things that annoy you: popping pills for every pain, munching junk food, smoking too much.

If you ever cross losers, they will fear you, but they won't forgive you. If they were tempted to be reasonable, they would put it off until it wouldn't do any good.

Some losers like to think they have legitimate excuses for failing. They talk about the economy, their health, their age, their bad luck, and their lack of intelligence.

These excuses don't convince me. Bad economy? We'll always have highs and lows; most people learn to live with both. Poor health didn't stop Franklin D. Roosevelt, who could have copped out because of his legs. Age didn't bother Grandma Moses, and it doesn't bother the girl or boy who brings your paper. Luck did not build General Motors, nor did it put anyone on the moon. If you say you lack intelligence, you're smarter than you think. I have worked with 36 millionaires who never went to college.

Successful people, superstars, don't make excuses. One of the big secrets of superstars is that they can even do what they really don't want to do: study an extra hour a day, get up at 4 A.M. to rework a plan, leave the gang at the bar an hour earlier.

Superstars are so different they may even seem odd. They seem illogical by way of ordinary thinking. Yes, they will sell when others cannot. They may be called irrational, because they demand and get top price.

The stars recognize that motivation is not permanent. "I eat three times a day," reasons the superstar, "so why shouldn't I renew my motivation?" Superstars keep up their fire.

The stars of today know that they must prospect, qualify, and close. They must also have willpower, memory, and imagination. In fact, 50 percent of their business comes from using their imagination. They realize that they must sell faster so they can see more people and close more prospects. As topflight sales personalities, they attempt to get the check from the buyer in the first ten minutes.

Strategies for a Winner

Superstars hold their good customers. They would advise these six strategies for a would-be winner:

1. *Be polite, pleasant, and cheerful.*
2. *Do first-class work.*
3. *Thank clients for their business.*
4. *Be a person of your word with follow-up service.*
5. *Keep calling year after year. Good customers are like good lodes in a mine. They don't play out. They fill your pockets.*
6. *It costs six times as much to get a new customer, so give your present customers plenty of tender, loving care.*

Superstars can be introverts or extroverts. They have a quiet intensity about achievement. They don't need a big audience; just one or two prospects will do. They never overwork or underwork. They just stay everlastingly at it. They are the shakers and doers who care little for preliminaries. They warm up, go into action, and keep rolling. Superstar salespersons are not very orthodox. They ride in on white horses, ready to take charge if necessary and save the company by selling enough to pay the bills.

They are aces. They sell like Number Ones and want to live like them: seven-bedroom homes, forty-foot cruisers, trips to Europe, fur coats. They have big dreams and big appetites for life. They have lots of friends, time off, and parties—and yet have minds like steel traps when it comes to business.

In other words, superstars are super in almost everything they do. They are tops in knowledge, tops in preparation, tops in character and personality, tops in drive, and above all, tops at finding and enjoying the best that life has to offer.

★★★★★★★★★ **CHAPTER 3** ★★★★★★★★★

Clock-Watching
Is for
Referees

Clock-watchers are a bit like the stooges who clamber up on stage and let a hypnotist put them to sleep with a slowly swinging watch. In a work setting, genuine clock-watchers can go to sleep looking at *any* nice, steady clock. I wouldn't be surprised if a real clock-watcher went to sleep watching a sundial.

Superstars use timepieces, but only as tools. They aren't mesmerized by them. Superstars are aware of the passage of time, but they value it so much they don't want to see it tick away. A superstar seller, like her brother on the gridiron, always seems to operate just as if the two-minute warning had been sounded.

Accomplished clock-watchers have one advantage over superstars: they get lots of sleep. Superstars are not asleep to the passage of time, so they organize it to work for them.

They know that organizing your time is actually a better way of getting needed sleep. After a well-organized day, you won't lie awake worrying about openings you couldn't close, appointments you didn't keep, questions you didn't answer, or fruitless arguments you didn't manage to avoid. You should also have the relaxed feeling that usually follows a full day of honest work.

The relaxed feeling must be the real thing, however, not an imitation. The clink of glasses with a boyfriend or a fast few rounds at the country club can be all right if the thirst quenching tops off a good day. After a bad day, however, the drinks are just a toast to failure, and the sweet music of relaxation is really just a poorly played requiem. Remember, Willy Loman's last sleep was forever.

Money, Brains, and Time

The superstar seller may be the head of a conglomerate or a one-person brokerage. Both of them need good management skills, and both need to understand Peter Drucker's formula for managing. Professor Drucker tells us that management has only three things to work with: money, brains, and time. The sole operator, just like the chief executive officer of a billion-a-year empire, has to juggle those same three key elements.

If you want to know which is the kingpin of these three magic ingredients, I absolutely believe it is time.

Money, of course, is useful when the hotel clerk sticks his hand out, the waiter brings the tab, or the printer sends his bill. Yet if you attempt to use it to replace honesty, punctuality, friendliness, and the knowledge of your product, you won't make the Super Bowl in selling.

Brains? Men and women who served in the armed forces can all tell you of the "90-day wonders" fresh out of college who couldn't get their brains into gear until the battle was lost. Brains can easily be shortcircuited by greed, dishonesty, egotism, laziness, and too big an appetite for food, liquor, and sex.

No, time is the one thing you can't do without. I am going to stress the use of time because if you use it well you'll soon have all the money you need to embellish your promotional efforts. Brains you must already have, or you'd be using this book as a door stopper instead of as the start of a thrilling career.

In selling, the person who squanders all three of Drucker's ingredients is a bum. The person who uses them to seek out a living is a seller. Those who mix all three intelligently enough to achieve their lifetime goals and fulfill the hopes of their teachers and friends are the superstars. If you are one of them, you are, according to the "80-20" principle, among the 20 percent who sell 80 percent of the world's goods and services. You are one in four; or, to put it another way, you are four times as effective as your fellow sellers.

If you are not in that bracket, you will be interested in how you can become four times more effecitive than you are now. If you should overshoot and become five times more successful, don't be alarmed. You've already bought this book, so your bookseller can't raise the price on you. If you borrowed it, you rascal, take it back to its owner and tell her how good it is.

The Greatest of These Is Time

The question of time has two aspects: how can you get more *of* it, and how can you get more *out of* the time you have? In a word (or two), you get more time by getting an earlier start in the day. You get more out of your day by sticking to a good schedule. I'll show you how to do both.

The Early Bird Gets the Orders

Although we don't want to be clock-watchers, we do have to take a look at some of the numbers on it. Let's look at 8 A.M., the time you want to be at work—in your home, at the office, or on the road. Why 8 A.M.? Well, the average seller, office worker, or manager gets to the day's place of business at 9 A.M. or later. If you want to be super, forget about what the average guy does.

What's that? You say you don't need to? Let me tell you a story. Recently, on the cruise ship *Norway*, I heard an authentic superstar in another bracket: the pianist Roger Williams. Such a performer, you would think, certainly did not need any practice, but practice he did, even on that floating resort. For him there was no breakfast in bed, no luxurious sleep-in of the pampered tourist. The only time he could get the use of the piano in the ship's Saga Theatre was from 2 A.M. until 8 A.M. So every day, this talented musician who could probably play "Chopsticks" with his toes, rolled out of bed by 1:30 A.M! Maybe we should call Mr. Williams not just a superstar but a super-superstar.

So now, let us not have any argument about starting work at 8 in the morning even if it means getting up at 6 A.M. to do it. If you have to get up at such an early hour, you will automatically have a free membership in the six o'clock club, an organization that includes some of this nation's most successful people. Although my own income is still only in the six-figure bracket, I am proud to maintain my membership as a six o'clocker.

Another longtime member who comes to mind is the late Arthur Godfrey, who charmed a national audience for years. No matter what time Godfrey awoke—5, 4, 3, even 2 A.M.—he got up and started working. A friend who, though retired, paid a six-figure income tax in 1983, once told me, "When I decided to make some money, I started getting up at six o'clock." (By the way, at 72 he still does it, and looks and acts like a 50-year-old. Superstars have a way of looking better. They are unusual in more ways than making money.)

When you start working at 8 A.M., you will discover an amazing thing: that 90 percent of the phones in America are not answered until after 9 A.M. All you get are rings or, if you wait long enough, a recording telling you, "We open at nine." You can't reach anyone in that first hour, and most likely no one will call you. But even if your phone is as quiet as a trout, there is still plenty to do in the wee hours: cleaning up the paperwork, planning the day's calls, listening to a tape, writing letters. If you can't think of anything to do until the loafers are at their desks, forget the superstar program and go back to bed.

Seriously, you really shouldn't give up on the 8 A.M. start even if at first you run out of things to do, because you will soon begin to make the hour count. It is going to be part of your edge on the just plain star. It is one of the steps to adding the word *super* to your classification.

What you want to do is form the habit of getting an hour's edge every day. You'll need some other good habits, but the 8 A.M. habit will help you acquire the others.

The Six-Day Method

To solidify this and the other habits you have only to practice the "six-day method." If you do something regularly for six days in a row, you will have accomplished the hardest part of good habit formation. (Bad habits, you can get in just one or two tries.)

I have used the six-day method with success although I read about it only about a month before I wrote these words. Perhaps my first success with it was to put my sitting-up exercises on a regular basis. For years I had been starting and stopping the morning sit-ups and other healthful "tortures." I made and broke resolutions like soap bubbles, but now I'm keeping at the morning exercises.

Another victory I won is in the writing of this book.

With 55,000 words as a working target, I knew that I would have to hit a steady pace to complete the task in the agreed period of six months. According to my simple arithmetic, 55,000 divided by 176 days meant a daily requirement of 312 words. With the expected interruptions, I realized that a heavier pace would be necessary, even on the road. So I set a target of 550 words on the days I could work at the project. I had to do it that way; otherwise I could look forward to a writing marathon as I neared the delivery date. I don't mind the keep-awake coffee, but I can't stand wearing toothpicks to keep my eyelids propped open.

Again the six-day method did the trick. I am now "hooked" on the writing schedule. If I have to miss a day or for some reason don't make my quota, I get right back at it at the first opportunity. I hope there is no cure for this addiction.

Good News About Sleep

Right about now, some of you may be wondering how you'll get up at 6 A.M. for even one day, let alone six. I can hear the groans from here. But let me give you some bad news/good news on the subject. The bad news is that there is a possibility that you sleep too much already. Eight hours is normal, but some need more, some less.

How can you tell? I would say that if you are reasonably healthy, weigh about what you should, and observe moderation in eating, drinking, and exercising, you are probably sleeping about as long as you should under present circumstances. After you start moving like a superstar, you may want an extra hour now and then; not every day, of course, but just when you need it.

The good news is that if you suspect you sleep too much, you can do something about it. If you are overweight, seldom exercise, and clink too many ice cubes, you may be overloading your system to the point where you need more sack time.

If you have not had a physical checkup lately, here's an item for tomorrow's schedule: call your doctor and make an appointment. If you check out okay, you should be able to go on a reasonable diet and start exercising. As for cutting down on drinking, you can do that without a doctor's okay.

Your doctor might find things that need correcting. He might even recommend a "sleep study" for you, especially if your spouse complains of your snoring. You could be one of the unfortunates who suffer from obstructed sleep apnea (OSA). The afflicted person actually stops breathing because of a malfunctioning breathing apparatus. I know of one sufferer who stopped breathing for a total of 30 minutes every hour during a six-hour sleep study. People with OSA are normally tired all day and are often not as sharp mentally as they should be. Their curtailed breathing deprives the brain of some of its oxygen needs.

Fortunately, sleep apnea and other maladies can be corrected. Dr. George Schossow of White Bear, Minnesota, used me a few months ago as a guinea pig for his improved method of doing the sleep study.

The next morning Doc replayed a portion of the videotape made of me during the night. The verdict? I didn't even snore enough to scare away the cat that had sneaked up on my bed during the night. Yet the sleep study was not a total loss. It told the trained ear of Dr. Schossow that I had asthma, something I did not realize and no doctor had ever discovered before. Doc prescibed the proper medicine, so now my nighttime breathing is much improved. Had I been one of those violent snorers with OSA, he had the medication for that, too. The patient who breathed only half the time at night now gets all the sleep he needs, and his next-door neighbors no longer can complain.

Once your doctor corrects what can be corrected and you improve your fitness, you may make the happy discovery that it gets easier to get up in the morning. You may also find that you get up earlier and take on the new day with more zest and optimism.

I woke up this morning at 5 A.M. and made the mistake

of trying to sleep another hour. No way. I ran out of sheep, but still couldn't make it. After 30 minutes of tossing, I finally rolled out, tidied up, did my exercises, and lit into the morning's chores. It is now 11:45 A.M., and I am hungry but certainly not sleepy. Last night I put the cat out at 11 P.M., and I am planning on letting her out to prowl about the same time tonight.

Superstars Start Early

Getting an early start on the day is typical of the superstar. By 9 A.M., when the middle-of-the-road person is just getting started, you will have had a good warm-up. The superstar ballet dancer and the professional athlete wouldn't dream of appearing without toning up the muscles and reflexes beforehand. When you start to deal with the conventional people, the nine-to-fivers, you should be charged up enough to score a victory—no, not just a victory but a victorious day.

But hold on a minute before we proceed with the victory march. I want you to consider my use of the term conventional in the previous paragraph. If you look up conventional in your *Webster*, you will find something like "sanctioned by, or growing out of custom or usage; customary; formal; not natural, original, or spontaneous."

In other words, you can be conventional without rocking any boats or raising any eyebrows. In fact, in recent years you can get away with a lot of things and still be conventional. You can lie, but, of course, you'll call it something like "managing the news" or "adjusting the facts." You can pad your expense account, rearrange your daily report, misrepresent yourself and your merchandise, hide your cash payments from the IRS. You can go out with a cabaret entertainer instead of making another call or doing your paperwork. You can do all these things and still pass for a conventional person. You can "get by" because "getting by" is now conventional: "Everyone's doing it."

In choosing to be a superstar you are pledging yourself to eliminate as many conventionalities as good sense and good behavior will permit. When you join the six-o'clock club or become an 8 A.M. starter, you already deserve the label *unconventional*.

Isn't it a good, exhilarating feeling? It should be, because you have taken the first step across the border of the state of mediocrity into the realm of the superstar.

So when I talk of a day of victory I mean a full day's work. Too many salespeople are not even mediocre. They just put in a few hours. No wonder they turn belly up. The superstar's day is 10, 12, maybe 14 hours, and, on rare occasions, even longer. I have frequently worked as long as 20 hours to meet certain deadlines.

There will be days when you can wrap up your tent a lot earlier than usual. If you have only one mansion among your listings and you sell it over morning coffee, you could hardly be censored if you called it a day. If, on the other hand, your dream sale has pumped the old adrenalin into your arteries, you might finish off the day by moving some smaller properties.

In any case, you must be unconventional enough to do what can and should be done, even though the little hand points straight down and the big hand straight up.

Of course, if someone—your wife or your husband—is expecting you, a quick phone call is in order. Being a superstar also requires thoughtful consideration of others, an attitude that should not be unconventional, but often is.

I recall a big operator whose fleet of trucks, brokerage business, and far-flung land holdings caused him to miss the family dinner far too often to suit his wife. When she said dinner was at six, she meant P.M. and not A.M. Unfortunately, my friend was not quite a superstar. He had the potential, but he just didn't touch all the bases when he thought he was scoring a home run. His divorce, I was told, cost him at least half a million. His other lapses into conventional behavior finally also cost him the control of his empire.

I cannot tell you how many hundreds of orders I have picked up at 5:30 P.M. by making extra phone calls or by keeping a late appointment. Just being ready to see people has opened doors for me—and closed sales.

To accommodate your occasional, justifiable breaches of family protocol you must come to an understanding beforehand. Of course, this is a two-way street in an increasing number of households today in which wives also face demands of business careers. When you must work late every now and then, suggesting a late dinner out often helps keep the domestic peace. If your client still needs more selling, why not bring him or her along?

Your family will more easily accept occasional lapses from the usual time schedule if you are as super at home as you are in your commercial life. Be extra thoughtful, extra courteous, and you can make everyone understand that you are borrowing a bit of time that will be repaid with interest.

Importance of a Daily Schedule

Scheduling is probably the most necessary weapon in your selling arsenal. It will help you get more out of the time you put in. Having a daily schedule should should help you avoid the frantic efforts that too many sellers make to catch up with quotas they or their sales managers have set.

Working out a schedule is one way to give yourself some goals for the day. And don't feel embarrassed about it. It is a lot better to be slavish to a schedule than to such pursuits as playing golf, elbow-bending, or watching sports and soap operas.

The actual physical form your schedule takes is up to you. I have developed a format called the Go Chart that works well for me (see sample at end of chapter). I'm one of those who likes to check things off a list after I've done them. You can use any method of planning your time and setting goals for your day, as long as you actually *do* it.

Developing a New Sense of Time

You already have one big secret to time management: get an early start. My second tip is just as easy: adopt the superstar's attitiude about time. Superstars always look for ways to make good, productive use out of every bit of time they have. You'll never hear them talking about "killing time"; they put it to work.

For example, let's say you have to attend a sales meeting in another city. Your husband drops you off at the airport on his way to work. Your plane doesn't leave until 11 A.M., but he has to drop you off at 8:30 to get to work on time. So, after checking in, you have more than two hours before you board the plane.

Then you spot a client who just a few months ago bought a ranch-style home for $150,000. You might think, "Oh Lord, I'll be just wasting my time if I visit with him. Maybe I can sit where he won't see me."

If you are just a time puncher and not a time user you would probably stay out of sight. If your thinking is superstar style, however, you might do a bit of what TV Pastor Robert Schuller calls "possibility thinking." Although your old client is now out of the house market—because you put him out of it—there may well be a day when he thinks of a summer home, a more expensive house, or possibly even a commercial building. So you walk up and ask him how he likes his house. If he frowns, you've got your parcel of time back again. If he smiles, you may have just laid the groundwork for a fat commission at a future date that could be sooner than you think.

To pursue this further, let us say you spend ten minutes engaging in pleasantries. Then he excuses himself to call his office. You won the waiting game. You gave up only a few minutes of your time to be nice to a future prospect, and you still have more than an hour and a half to yourself.

You could use that time reading a magazine, taking a nap, or writing cards to friends. But you should consider whether these activities fit the situation—namely that you really are at work. If you were not waiting for a plane, you would be at your phone trying to make an appointment with a prospect who has shown interest in a warehouse, the listing of which has only three weeks to run. Here, then, is the key to your time use.

When I have an hour to get ready for an interview I use ten minutes reviewing my knowledge of the product, property, or service I hope to sell. The lion's share, 50 minutes, I use to plan my closing strategy. If you already know every detail about the building in question, you can use the waiting time to plot out a closing strategy.

Then, before long, you get on the plane. Let us put you in the no-smoking section next to a doctor and his wife who are on their way to an orthopedic conference. They are friendly, so you visit.

Are you wasting time while you chat? Of course not. For you, getting to the meeting is what you are supposed to be doing. If you had something pressing for your attention, you would have explained your problem and gone to work on it. Since you are just going to attend the meeting as a listener, you might as well relax.

On the other hand, if your seatmates are absorbed in their own concerns, count your blessings. If the warehouse sale, your only immediate problem, is well in hand after your planning session back at the terminal, you are entitled to relax. If you have superstar blood in your veins, what you choose for enjoyment will most likely also be profitable.

Time-Wasters

You're on the plane, on your way to a sales meeting and because you're a superstar, I know you have some substantial goals in view: to learn a new technique or new markets, to fire up your enthusiasm, or maybe just to find out if you are doing things right. However, we are talking about time, and using it wisely, and so I am conscience-bound to post a warning about meetings, which I once heard defined as "things at which minutes are taken and hours are lost."

In some enterprises, both profit and nonprofit, meetings are a way of life. Almost everything has to be decided at a meeting. Some matters that should be handled over the phone—or forgotten entirely—are too often the occasion for a meeting. We have all attended meetings where no one brought any information to speak of: no position paper, no guidelines, no facts.

My worst meeting was one I volunteered to attend. What I had really volunteered for was a planning committee, a project I thought the organization sorely needed. The chairperson told the group, about 15 divisional managers, that our purpose was to make a map of our respective territories. Never mind that we already had such a map.

As the meeting developed it was apparent that no one had even a remote idea what we were expected to use for territorial borders—rivers, roads, meridians, or imaginary lines. Someone then called the home office and was told to respect the old borders as much as possible but to "make such alterations as would reflect changes in responsibilities and areas of action."

When the dinner break was called, I made a break for an exit instead. I don't think anyone missed me. I am certain, though, that the new map was never finished. It was missed even less than I was.

Some people think they are working when they sit in a meeting, no matter how boring it is. Of course, meetings are not the only time-consumers, but they can be insidious hour-wasters simply because they are considered to be worthwhile work even when the chairs are comforting and the agenda confusing.

What I call "getting lost in the woods" is another big time-waster. Distractions can be almost as fruitless as an unnecessary meeting. The friendly tavern is one of the first.

The first venture into the fascinating distractions of the seemingly friendly forest is usually just a fleeting experience. An old friend suggests a quick one. Before long, you agree to be an officer in your lodge or club, you invest in a new venture that "will run itself," you expand your weekend golf just a little bit, or you fill in your lunch hour with a fast game of rummy.

Once you get into the edge of this forest, your next steps take you a bit further. The quick one becomes two (and the barmaid starts to look better), the lodge job calls for more extra meetings (and what better place than where what's-her-name works), the sideline venture calls for interesting some new capital ("Give these guys a drink, Dolly"), your Wednesday afternoon golf games get you acquainted with a young doctor ("Hey, honey, I just dropped by to have you meet Doc Jones"), you move the card game to a place with more privacy ("Dolly, honey, bring us another round").

Before you get really lost in the forest, set yourself up a schedule and stick to it. Get used to saying, "Sorry, boys, I am scheduled for one o'clock," but for heaven's sake have something scheduled for one o'clock. It may be just to call the Welcome Wagon lady to get the names of new people who moved to town. If some Nosy Parker says, "What for?" you can honestly say, "It's a little complicated. I'll explain later." Chances are your questioner wouldn't understand if you did explain. You can be sure he'll forget it before the next deal.

Not only does a schedule protect you from your own weakness, but it also helps bring home to you just how much time there really is in a day when you organize it. There is even plenty of time for good deeds and fun too. Getting organized helps you do them at the right time and in the right way. If you want to ascend to the status of a superstar, you must treat your schedule as you do your American Express card: Don't leave home without it.

You are not going to produce a perfect schedule on the first try, but you will soon get the hang of it. For openers, check my Go Chart later in this chapter. Very likely you can use it as is. It will help keep you aware of the things a seller has to do each day as a seller. Some of the items are for mere survival. Some are for climbing the ladder of success. The most important items are to keep you climbing where the ordinary ladder ends and the superstar cliff begins.

Mail to Customers

It may seem like putting the cart way before the horse, but the first piece of business that should go on your schedule is the writing of thank-you notes. Number 5 on my Go Chart is "Mail to old customer." If you don't send anything else to someone you have just sold, at least thank him. And do it in writing. Everyone likes to get mail. A phone call is nice, but, unless the recipient records it, it can be heard only once. I knew the president of a small air service who couldn't spell. No one got personal notes from him. No one gets on his airplanes anymore either.

When you write your personal thanks, you say a lot of things: you appreciate the business; you can read and write; and you are an unusual person, very likely a superstar. The fact that so few people take the trouble even to say "thank you," much less write it, is something that sets you apart from the common herd. Believe me, the more you can set yourself apart from the crowd, the more likely you will wind up leading it.

Of course, this thank-you business is usually good for only one try. If you have put 30 minutes on your schedule for writing letters, you can quickly take care of the gratitude notes—unless you had a very good day or week. There are a lot of other things you can write to an old customer. You may not have seen him in a year, but there is always something to justify a letter or even just a card. When you are on vacation you send cards to your friends, so why not to your customer? If he isn't a friend, who is? When an old customer gets a promotion or an appointment to serve as an official or committee member of a lodge, wins a tournament, or is cited in the press for something worthwhile, your handwritten congratulations will be in order. Even a dictated letter will serve the purpose.

Let's face it, part of the reason you write a note of any kind to a customer is to insure her or his allegiance to your cause. Don't, however, let this show in your note or letter. I recall a banker who "shot himself in the foot" when he tried to give a three-gun salute to a customer who had just received a statewide honor. Moneybags wrote five well-worded paragraphs about the achievement and about the honor that it brought to the community. The last paragraph, however, was a masterpiece in the *faux pas* department: "By the way, I've noticed that you haven't made any deposits lately in your savings account. Why don't you drop in one of these days, and we can talk about it?"

At certain times of the year you may have to fatten the time allotment for writing. So get some extra help if you have to for Christmas greetings.

A Minnesota man who owns seven motels had a terrific idea. Night clerks—who usually have time on their hands—are given the job of sending out Christmas cards to all the customers. Each envelope contains a $2 coupon to be applied against future lodging bills. It has worked so well that the clerks now insert another coupon for a friend of the client. This small lodging chain sends out 60,000 Christmas cards every year. This promotion was so effective that the owner was able to eliminate a $10,000 expenditure in the Yellow Pages.

Ideas are fruitful. They increase and multiply. That is why imagination is such an important ingredient in super-star selling. If you have it, use it. If you don't have it, try to develop it.

Plan Your Free Time

My next schedule suggestion may seem as odd as the first one: figure out what you should do with your free time. One of the things that distinguishes a superstar is the way he or she spends the nonworking hours. In truth, the battle in selling is won by what you do between 5 P.M. and 8 A.M. the next morning. This is free time, but it isn't wasted time.

To begin with, it's a question of attitude. Too many have the idea that in addition to a living, the world also owes them a good time. This is a terrible misinterpretation of our legacy from the Founding Fathers: "life, liberty, and the pursuit of happiness." I am sure they meant "the right to do the things that earn happiness."

That is what your free time is for, perhaps even more than your working hours. Leisure is not an end in itself but a means. To get anything out of your leisure you have to fit it into your life plan.

Once you get the superstar's attitude toward the importance of goal setting, you can skip the detailing of your free time activities. A genuine superstar could almost put down just one thing on his relaxation agenda: "Five P.M. to 8 A.M.: Do as much as possible to make myself a better person."

Doing what comes naturally may seem to be the superstars' way of approaching things, work or play. Really though, they had to push themselves past an imaginary line, the line that weaker folks would regard as the breaking point.

A bus driver I once knew gave up his job rather than miss the opening of deer season. He found it easier to get his deer than another job. People like that just are not destined for the *Guinness Book of Records*. Neither will you be if you pattern your life on those whose only commandment is "Do what everyone else is doing."

You do not exactly have to be a trailblazer to be a superstar. Others have passed up cocktails at the club to get home to the family, or read a good book instead of watching sports or a game show, or took a walk instead of making a big fat sandwich. You will not be a pioneer when you do these things, but you will be different, unconventional, someone set apart. Others may laugh at you, but you will be so far ahead of them you won't even hear their cackle.

When you organize your free time schedule, you put a large part of your life in order. You should have at least an hour for reading or listening to tapes, whatever amount of time is necessary to produce letters that sell, and enough minutes to keep your paperwork current.

If you utilize your free time better, you will not only enjoy your leisure more, but you will use your work hours more effectively. You may even find yourself having some fun just doing a better job every day.

If you have followed your leisure schedule to the best of your ability, you should have little trouble with your workday. Tell me how you spend your spare time, and I will tell you what your income will be.

For some specific ideas, take a look at the Go Chart. Several of the items can easily be done during your free time: 1, daily schedule; 8, reading today; 9, six o'clock club; 14, total goal for the month; 15, one extra hour of sleep; and 16, review the day. A few others can sometimes be done at home: 2, asking for referrals; 4, 5, mail to old and new customers; 7, appointments tomorrow; 12, phoning; and 13, pep or faith talks (once in a while there is something worthwhile on the airwaves, but I am thinking more of tapes). By the way, some of these things can also be done in your hotel room or in various reception rooms you use while waiting for your clients.

Putting the Phone to Work for You

When you start your workday you must have from two to five firm appointments if you are going to be a contender in that arena that Robert Ringer calls "the jungle." And to have the appointments you need to make decent sales, you will have to make a lot of phone calls. One and a half to two hours should handle it. Whether you are in your store or on the road, you will have plenty to call about.

In your store you should be calling to check on your customers' satisfaction with big-ticket items. If you sold a

Sheehan's Go Chart *Answer Yes or No, or Actual Figures Daily*

		1	2	3	4	5	6	7	8	9	10	11	12	13	14	15	16	17	18	19	20	21	22	23	24	25	26	27	28	29	30	31
1	Daily Schedule — 15 to 30 Min. Daily																															
2	Referrals — Ask																															
3	Presentations with Close																															
4	Mail to new Customer																															
5	Mail to old Customer																															
6	Appointments today																															
7	Appointments tomorrow																															
8	Reading today																															
9	6 O'Clock Club																															
10	Daily Quota																															
11	Sold Today																															
12	Phone Calls Today																															
13	Pep Talks or Faith Talks																															
14	Total Goal for Month																															
15	One Extra Hour Sleep																															
16	Review Day																															

My Closing Average for This
Month is _____

"The best salespeople in America failed two or three times before they realized the big secret in business — Organize Yourself Daily." — Don Sheehan

Don Sheehan's Courses

5001 Belmont Avenue South
Minneapolis, Minnesota 55419
(612) 338-6739

mobile home, find out how the new owner likes it, and also ask if the buyer knows anyone else who might be interested in something similar.

You sold a lot of rugs three years ago? Fine; now call the buyers about cleaning jobs. Again, if you install something, check to see (1) if everything is satisfactory, (2) if installers left everything in good order, and (3) if they showed up on time, or at all.

The phone will also help you collect bills. Although our society protects the slow payer or nonpayer almost more than it does the seller, you can still phone during business hours. Instead of harassing your debtor, you might volunteer to come over to pick up the check.

During the 1930s my father spent some time collecting the bills owed to a large firm. At one home he could never find the husband home so he pleaded for payment with the wife. After six or eight calls the lady finally told my father, "You'll just have to quit calling. The neighbors are beginning to talk."

Unless you make from 25 to 50 phone calls a day, you will no longer be a breadwinner. You may not have time to call all the people you haven't seen in a year. No problem. Have someone do it for you. Jean and Paula Sheehan make from 500 to 1,000 calls a month for me.

Save Time for the Sabbath

Along with each individual day, you also have to budget your month. If you can manage it, try for a five-day week. That means 23 working days. If you have to, you include Saturdays to give you a 27-day month. However, making calls is more difficult on Saturday.

Whatever you do, you should have a Sabbath, Sunday for some, Saturday for others. Stay with the Sabbath idea. The people I have seen prospering and enjoying a superstar life-style were faithful to the Lord's Day.

Schedule Success

Your schedule will help you if you are willing to do the things that help you follow it. It will keep you conscious of your need to read things that will inform you and stimulate you. You need your schedule to help you stay healthy enough to do superstar work and live a superstar life.

To make any schedule work you will have to do three simple things. They are (1) start it, (2) keep at it, and (3) finish it.

These can be accomplished if you use your clock or your watch for only two things: to get up early and to keep appointments. It is the players, not the timekeepers, who are the superstars.

CHAPTER 4

There's Gold in Them Thar Hills

A farmer has a piece of land. A cobbler has a shop. A manufacturer has a factory and the raw material out of which the product will be made. As a seller you also have raw materials to put to use, but many of them are invisible. The "stuff" you have to work with is what's inside you, the kind of person you are, and the way you deal with your customers. You can decide to take advantage of this raw material, to build things with it and make it pay, or you can leave it untapped.

It's like the hills of South Dakota. The early inhabitants of this region made use of the natural resources, but not nearly as well as they could have. They set up homesteads, but they either didn't know about, or didn't care much about, the precious metals buried in the earth. Then one day a prospector discovered the gold, and knew what to do with it. Today, South Dakota is one of our nation's strongest gold-producing states.

Your customers are your gold mine. How you treat them, how you behave, how you conduct yourself as an inhabitant of this planet, will determine whether your mine pays off, or peters out.

To survey your own personal mine, check your records. If you have 50 good, steady customers who bring you an average of $750, they will be worth $37,500 a year to you. Suppose you are 35 years old. If you are successful at holding these customers until you retire at 65, you will have accumulated a total of $1.125 million.

The sum total of your prospecting gives you what amounts to a capital base of over $1 million. How many small businesses are capitalized at that figure? The nice thing about building up this capital base is that you can do a lot of it at no cost to you. You can get a lot out of your gold mine with free "tools" that you already have, even though they may be a bit rusty.

Courtesy and Honesty

Courtesy is always a winner. Don't underestimate its effect. You will have much more success selling people if you treat them kindly and with decency. Recently I stopped in at Marshall Field's in Chicago to buy a tie and a matching handkerchief. It wasn't much of an order, but the clerk was so cheerful, so courteous, so gracious that I complimented her. Where do you think I'll go shopping the next time I'm in Chicago?

Another free tool is honesty. If you have heard it once, you have heard it a thousand times: "Honesty is the best policy." To some that statement is a challenge to find an easier or more effective way of getting somewhere—truthful or not. Give them a job description stating that lying is the best policy, and they would go along with it.

Truth should really be more than a policy with you. It should be the framework of your character. Telling the truth should be as automatic as pulling back your hand when you touch a hot stove.

To stimulate your own memory of instances where built-in honesty paid off, I'd like to tell you about Joe McDougal, who made a fortune through plain, simple honesty.

Joe was a superstar seller who believed that what he had to sell would be valuable to the buyer: shares in a company that he was sure could not miss. When Joe had sold about $200,000 worth of the shares, he learned that he had been hoodwinked, neatly and completely. The stock he had sold was as worthless as a ticket to Atlantis.

Although he had acted in good faith as a seller, Joe knew that a lot of folks who had trusted him were losing money they could not spare. He also knew that swindlers are slow payers, to say the least. If anyone was going to be repaid, it was up to Joe McDougal to do it, and do it he did. His absolute honesty earned him the credibility and the credit that enabled him to recoup his fortune. It took many years of hard work to finish the task, but when he completed the repayments his credit was as good as the government's. Maybe better.

Listening

A third valuable tool is knowing how to listen, *really* listen.

I learned long ago that listening is usually more difficult than speaking. Years ago I had to learn enough Spanish to put my ideas across to the migrant workers from Texas who could handle only a few words in English. When I talked to them I used the words and expressions that hard work had put into my vocabulary. When they talked to me, however, it was a much different story. Their vocabularies included far too many words that were out of my range. When I talked, I was in command of my list of words. When they talked, I was at their mercy. You cannot very well hand your listeners a list of acceptable words and tell them to confine themselves to it.

When you are selling something, you know what you have to say, if you don't you shouldn't be trying to sell. But you won't get very far if you do all the talking. You also have to do your best to find out what is in your client's mind. Your prospect may be interested in an Oriental rug while you try to sell her wall-to-wall carpeting.

It would be better to offer "a penny for your thoughts" as an interview opener than to launch a high-pressure spiel that swamps your listener. A bigger danger is that you won't hear the buyer signals if you keep talking. If your client just about knows what she wants, she won't talk a lot. If you are listening with your mind as well as your ears, you will hear your customer say, "I know what I want. If you have it at a decent price, I'll buy it. In fact, even if the price is a bit nasty, I'll take it if I can get it right now."

Some people interrupt continuously. What they tell their listeners is, "What you are trying to say isn't as important as what I'm going to tell you." Conversational interrupters do not really care whether their remarks are on the subject or not. They will even interrupt when you try to answer one of their questions. They seem to time their rudeness for the moment of your punch line or the point of your opinion. They do not really care what you have to say. It could be a side-splitting story, a stock tip, anything. Their ears are for their own voices. They need no other music.

Interruptions in a casual conversation may not be critical, but if you do this to a client, you will do only one thing of any value: you will save wear and tear on your cash register.

I recall one instance some years ago when a close friend was having financial difficulties. His business was sound because it provided a service that no one else attempted in his trade area. Somehow I convinced myself that my like-able buddy could make things work with a modest infusion of cash. But I did not get the opportunity to offer to help. He talked through my moment of weakness. My generosity ebbed away as he kept on talking trivialities. I was ready to offer gold, but he was interested in sawdust. No listening; no loan. My friend soon lost the business.

Courtesy, honesty, and the ability to listen are the essential tools for working your gold mine. There are some other useful ones—a photographic memory, unusual voice quality, a sense of humor—but not everyone has these gifts. The three big ones are available to everyone. They're free. And they are also priceless.

Incidentally, if you have a staff, part of your role as leader and manager is their training and guidance. It is your job to show them the value of these tools, as well as to use them yourself.

Persistence—itself a free tool—will help you obtain the attainable skills. You can work at being reliable. You can develop helpfulness. You can teach yourself—and your em-ployees—to be considerate.

Do It Now

If you really want to sharpen your skills with these tools, you will need, above all, one thing that you can't beg, borrow, or steal: the "do it now" habit. You must scratch "mañana" from your vocabulary. By taking care of today, you won't be have to worry about tomorrow.

To be courteous, you must start right now to learn to hold on to your temper. To be honest, you have to be truthful with yourself this very minute: admit faults you know you possess, but also recognize strong points that can be further developed.

If you want something to be difficult, put it off until later today. If you want it to be impossible, put it off until tomorrow.

Free Information

There is one more free tool that will help you get the best use out of the others—an active mind. The best way I know of to give your brain some exercise is to read (or, in our electronic age, listen to tapes). Not only do you give your brain cells a workout, but you can learn a lot.

Many of us have in our homes and offices books and tapes that we seldom use. We got them as gifts or bought them under the spell of a passing enthusiasm. Some of them may be junk. If so, give them to the Boy Scouts for their paper drive. If they are loaded with useful information—books of Peter Drucker and Frank Bettger, or tapes by Dennis Waitley—then use them. (If you coax enough I'll tell you about my books, *Shut Up and Sell* and *How to Get Your Prices,* and about my numerous tapes on selling, management, and motivation.)

Of course, your public library will have volumes that few private collectors could afford or have space for. I have found that when you have some spare time in a strange city it is better to have a thirst for knowledge than for the grape. In the long run, our thirst for knowledge is a lot less expensive to quench than the other kind. When I have time between appointments, I like to browse in bookstores or enjoy a bit of peace and quiet in a library.

Naturally, your reading and listening interests will lead you to the business shelves, but you should try not to be too narrow in your outlook. At least read one of the golden books of our civilization: the Bible, Torah, Talmud, or Koran. My daily choice is the Bible. My denomination pushes it more than the others.

Incidentally, my day starts with reading one chapter from the Old Testament and ends with a chapter from the New Testament. I do sitting-up exercises before I do any reading, but the sit-ups are just to get me geared up to start the real day of productive work. If you read your chosen golden book faithfully, you will quickly learn that genuine religion is not out to get your money, but to give you something. Like maybe some new tools.

CHAPTER 5

The Letter Carrier Is Your Bird Dog

Most successful duck hunters depend heavily on their highly trained bird dogs. If you drop a duck in the bullrushes, you could conceivably find it eventually, but a good dog will bring your dinner back in minutes. A bird dog, in other words, picks up something to which you have a claim.

A well-conceived letter can act like a bird dog for you. You can use it to flush out new prospects, or to retrieve old customers who have fallen in the marsh grass.

Writing to Old Customers

We already talked about budgeting time for thank-you notes, greetings, and the like. You can also use mail effectively to reestablish contact with clients you haven't seen for a while. Of course you could eventually get to every one of them, but you have only so much time for phoning and face-to-face visits. You can reach practically all your old clients with just one mailing. Make your letter friendly and personal, and my bet is you'll get good results.

This is another situation in which superstars excel. A surprising number of businesses make no attempt to find out why good customers disappear. You could be making so much money that you let your old customers go without a struggle. In that case you have wasted too much time on this book. In fact you could write your own sales guide: *How I Did $100,000 Worth of Business Without Repeat Business.*

Using Mail to Develop New Business

It should be obvious that you can effectively use mail to find new business. For my type of selling, it is an absolute necessity. I have to use mail to reach my multi-city audience. I operate regularly in such widely scattered places as Seattle, Las Vegas, Denver, Minneapolis, Fargo and Grand Forks, North Dakota; Rochester, Minnesota; and Stevens Point, Wisconsin. Lecturing assignments take me to Chicago, Atlanta, Fort Lauderdale, Orlando, and I have given training courses in several Canadian provinces.

To advertise adequately through the mass media in all the places I work would be far too expensive. Also, I would be paying for much more coverage than I need. My training courses are business-oriented, and my prospective audience is in the Yellow Pages.

Even if I could afford to use the mass media, I still would steer clear of that approach. A mass response would give me a massive headache. My courses are tailored to small, manageable groups of alert people who are serious about improving their merchandising skills. By using the mails I can canvass the people who are likely to want my services.

Planning Your Mailing Campaign

If I've succeeded in convincing you that mail makes sense, you may be tempted to sit down and start scribbling your letter right away. But first you should spend some time planning: who is going to get the mailing, when will it go out, how many pieces will you mail, and how much should you budget for it?

I know by experience just about how many mailing pieces I must send out to wind up with a profitable audience. To justify holding a sales seminar in Omaha, for example, I must have enough students to pay the following expenses:

1. Airline tickets—usually two, as my daughter Paula generally accompanies me to serve as hostess and sell my cassettes and books.

2. The cost of the mailing. Remember, mail should be considered a capital investment. It still is an investment in the future even if I do not get enough response to justify the trip. The solid responses are a workable lode for the future.

3. Rooms and meals for at least two persons, and refreshments for my classes.

4. Incidentals, which vary trip by trip, such as phone calls home or to my office, tips, and personal appearance items.

After expenses are met, I must not forget the reason for my trip: making a firm, steady step toward my annual goal of at least $100,000 a year, net. Include a profit in your budget.

As to when to mail, and to how many, I'll send you back to Chapter 3. Here's where your schedule comes in. The Go Chart does not say "every month," but that is what it means about "Mail to old customer," and "Mail to new customer." It also means a minimum of 1,000 pieces of mail. You might have to increase the number of letters assigned to each employee. Experience will tell you how much more than the minimum you need to keep things humming.

Writing a Good Letter

In using mail to discover new prospects you must always keep in mind that you are competing with a lot of giants who flood the postal service with their slickly prepared pitches. Don't be overpowered. Your market is made up of people who know what they want and how to get it. They are not swayed by the fast pitch, but they will listen to the genuine appeal of someone who presents something of value. Could a superstar sell anything else?

Basically, your letter should give an idea of what you have to offer, why the client should buy it, and why she should purchase it from you. It doesn't have to be cleverly worded. In fact, if your words are too slick they could convey the impression that you are a con artist. Excite curiousity, not suspicion.

The first sentence is the most critical part of the letter. If you can't catch the reader's attention with the opening sentence, you probably have lost your audience. On the other hand, if you can open with some informative attention grabber, you will likely wind up with an inquiry card or a phone call. Rewrite your letter a dozen times. Show it to someone who has to make a living by writing radio commercials, speeches, news articles, or sales letters and the like.

Test Mailings

Once you sweat out something that pleases a few advisers, including your spouse, test it. If it is tailored to new customers, send it out with a suitable reply card enclosed.

To make an adequate test run, you should be able to manage with 1,000 units.

If you get responses from 2 percent of your mailing pieces, you have a good letter on your hands. Twenty prospects should keep you busy for at least a week or longer if you have to make callbacks. You may even get referrals from the people you interview.

Not all your mail will make it all the way to its destination. Americans move around a lot. Some of your letters or cards may even die in wastebaskets. Don't worry. If you send out a properly written letter to enough people, you will invariably secure enough responses. The answers will provide you with all the leads you need until your next mailing.

Making Your Letter Look Good

The presentation of your letter can be almost as important as what it says. Sometimes the appearance of your letter is all it takes to swing a buyer in your direction.

The Personal Touch

Even though you are sending the same piece to perhaps thousands of people, you still want to project a feeling of personal contact with each individual. One of the best ways to do that is to address them by name wherever possible.

To accomplish this easily you may want to make another capital investment in your own future: a word processor. Mine cost me $4,250 plus a small investment in floppy discs needed to store information. It is worth every penny.

I am certain you can, as I did, find a business supply house that will put you on a monthly payment basis. For me, $275 a month worked out just fine. That extra amount to cover every month added to my motivation, and who cannot use a bit more of that?

Shop around a bit, and decide what features are important to you. I chose a model that produces clear, sharp typescripts, has more than enough memory capacity, and is backed by good service, both from the home office and from my supplier. Be sure you get a good, sturdy machine with an ironclad service policy. A word processor is a complicated machine that requires special skills to repair.

You will find that personalizing the salutations of your letters is but one of the many functions your machine performs, such as storing promotional letters and maintaining lists of new and old customers. As you or your typist become more familiar with your machine you will discover more new uses for it. I find new uses right along, including storing the corrected manuscript of this book.

If you are still in the process of building your resources, you may have to curtail your investment, but as soon as you can, don't hesitate to move into the fantastic world of the future, which in many respects is already here.

You may prefer to use a secretarial service. I continue to employ such a service to handle the overload when my own equipment is crowded to the limit. Of course with a service you can tailor letters to various types of prospects.

You can also use memory-capable typewriters to write to new prospects. If you do not know their names, you can still give your letter a personal touch by using the probable title of the person you are addressing. For example:

Acme Mobile Home Sales
P.O. Box E 48
Wichita Falls, TX 76301

Dear Sales Manager:

You can leave the address in the memory for both your current letter and possible future use.

The use of a title helps get around the awkward expression, "Dear Sir or Madam." If there is no other way around it, use the clumsy salutation. It is better to stumble around a bit than fall flat on your face with a chauvinistic expression.

Hand Addressing Your Envelopes

Another very effective way to create a personalized feeling is to address your envelopes by hand. Sure it takes time, but I have found that it gets more people to open the letter. Which is really the name of the game.

When you have the option of automatically typing a list of names from a memory bank, you may be tempted to skip the labor of handwriting. Do a test mailing with the auto-typing. If you can reduce your cost per response, then go for it. Of course, if the number of replies is too small, you defeat your purpose. You must have those leads.

Go First Class

Special touches like hand addressing and personal salutations really are worth the extra effort. They mark the difference between professional and amateur mailings. The difference in impression on the receiver is a lot like the difference between first class and tourist on the airlines.

So my advice is, go first class whenever you can. Including the postage itself. It may seem tempting to use the lower-cost bulk mailings, but when the post office is overloaded with first-class mail, the third-class letters have to wait. To unearth leads that will be followed by personal attention, first-class mail is the best.

CHAPTER 6

Your Phone
Should Give You
Two Good Rings

Probably nothing so aptly symbolizes a successful, busy office like the sound of ringing phones. It is up to you to make certain that your ringing phones make your cash registers ring too. How you, or your employees, use the phone is going to gain or lose business for you.

You have to be sure your phone system is adequate, that you and your people know how to use the equipment, and that your phone manners are the best they can be.

Phone Power

Not long ago I was in a local department store to buy about $200 worth of draperies, and I needed a salesperson. When I finally found one, she never stayed with me very long at a time because she had to run back every few minutes to answer the phone. After about the third interruption I thought, "That's the way to do it. Get 'em on the phone!"

You *must* have phone power. Without it you are not going to make it in America—not with today's cost for road transportation. You think gasoline is expensive? The price of gas is really the *good* news when you account for all your per-mile costs. Even if you buy a used car from "Honest John" and save on repairs at your local garage, it's going to cost at least 30 cents per mile to run your car.

When you put a quarter in the slot to call instead of driving a mile, you save five cents. I do not want you to become a penny-pincher, but I would hate to see you become a penny-pitcher either. I understand that pitching pennies is popular with people who have nothing better to do.

Of course, if you *have* to drive to do the job, then that's what you do—even if it costs a dollar a mile. If you have to hire a limousine to make a sale, don't hesitate. Still, you are going to have more expense money at your command if you use the phone judiciously. I have known far too many people who have made 70- and 80-mile trips without phoning ahead to make sure their client was going to be in. Maybe they have time to waste like that, but superstars don't.

Actually, it is still a good idea to phone ahead even if you know your client will be in. There is, of course, the possibility that your call might give your prospect time to build up sales resistance. On the other hand, she might decide before you arrive that what you have is just what she needs, and you could walk in on a buyer who has already sold herself. So you close, say goodbye, and head for the nearest phone to call the next prospect.

Modern Phone Equipment

We've come a long way since Alexander Graham Bell called
Mr. Watson to come and lend a hand. Today's phone user
has so many new options that few, if any, know how to use
all of them.

Answering Machines and Other Helpers

I used an answering device for many years, but I now
prefer an answering service. Most people would rather
reach a live voice than a canned message. My friend Al
"Skinhead" Grivno, in fact, gets downright upset. And with
his pungent vocabulary, he could make a drill sergeant
blush. When he got my recorded message instead of me, he
blew out a fuse or two. On a good try he could blow out the
whole neighborhood.

Yet if no answering service is available—and Skinhead
doesn't live near you—you can sometimes make good use of
your answering machine. Even if you have a phone operator there may be occasions when you do not want to be
reached. Just turn on your machine and let it take the
undesired calls. You or your phone operator can break in if
it happens to be someone you want to talk to—even Skinhead.

Lest I give an unfair impression of Skinhead, this is the
comment of his son Steve, partner in Al's Body Works in
Crookston, Minnesota: "Dad, you make more money on the
phone then I do bending fenders."

Another good use of your phone recorder is to stand
guard for after-hours calls. After all, if your clients know
they can reach you day or night, they will prefer you to
someone who sticks to office hours. For those customers
who provide the lion's share of your business—the 20 percent who put 80 percent of the bread on your table—you
may want to do more. Give them a special card inviting
them to use your round-the-clock phone monitoring. An

unlisted number for your very best clients would not be out of order. It will give them a feeling that they are special—which they are. Don't worry, your best customers won't bother you with extra calls any more than Andropov, in his day, bothered President Reagan over the most famous of all hotlines.

Your reliable accounts are also "80/20" clubbers in another way: they give you 80 percent of your business but require only about 20 percent of your time and expense. The customers who provide you with only 20 percent of your receipts will invariably soak up 80 percent of your time and expense money.

Another modern phone device I own is a cordless phone. I always keep it hooked up ready to use, especially at home. When I am expecting an important call I keep my portable phone right on my person. It has a good hearty roar. If I don't hear it, the neighbors across the street come over and pound on my door in protest. In fact, I sometimes carry it over to my friends' houses, and then *their* neighbors complain.

Is Your System Adequate?

You've probably all been in restaurants or clubs where the management tried to get by with too few waiters. Sure they save on personnel costs, but they always lose out on sales or revenue-producing drinks. Make sure you don't fall into this trap of false economy with your phone system. If your phones are ringing too much (really, they can never ring too often), you may need another unit and another operator.

When is your system overloaded? If a caller gets a busy signal once in a while, don't worry. That can even be good for you; one busy signal tells the caller that your enterprise is good enough to be in demand. Two busy signals might suggest that someone in your place is a bit long-winded. Three or four failures to make contact could very easily set your caller thinking about trying another vendor. Maybe not, if the caller is your friend; remember, you will never have too many friends as a seller.

You can test for overloading—and a lot of other things—by calling your office when you have to be out. You will do yourself a favor if you discover a need for more phones.

If you have an incoming WATS line you are in a different position with respect to callers. They have the option of hanging up and trying later, or they can hold their place in line by sitting tight. I would ask you to think twice, however, about installing the systems that play music for waiting callers. I hate it, you hate it, and probably your customers do too.

As a working rule, I would say do not answer more phones than your operators can handle right away. An answering device promising a callback would probably be acceptable, but study the results. If what you do with your phones keeps you busy closing sales, forget the study.

Phone Manners

No matter what kind of phone you use, there is the big question of how you use it. Number one problem: phone-aholics. If you have a teenager at home, you know what a phone-aholic is. They don't feel secure unless it rings and rings for them. When they answer they don't know what to say—but keep on talking anyway. Neither you nor anyone working for you should indulge in this practice.

Another big problem: the phone trapper. I am sure you have experienced phone-trapping. It happens when you get someone on the line who does not want to get off. You may have a plane to catch, and you tell them. It makes no difference. Their filibuster continues. If the phone-trapper wanted to give you some earth-shaking information, it would not be so bad. The trouble is, the quality of the phone trapper's chatter is in inverse proportion to its length. The longer the talk, the emptier the outpouring.

I once worked an experiment with a notorious phone pest. I knew by experience that even hanging up did no good. I also knew that there would not be anything useful coming out of the earpiece. I set the phone down on my desk and left the room for at least three minutes. When I got back the instrument was still cackling.

The Sound of Your Voice

Have you ever paid attention to how you sound? Some would rate the bored, listless voice even worse than the stuck-record type. You—or whoever answers your phone— should listen to your voice sometimes. If you sound bored to yourself, how will you sound to customers?

Another thing to consider is your telephone voice projection. If you prefer mumbling to speaking, have someone else do your phoning. Better yet, learn how to enunciate. Not everyone in the world is as used to the way you talk as your spouse. And hearing problems are more common than you might think.

When I have to listen to a mumbler I do the best I can. For maybe the first five minutes I ask for a repetition of the statement. When I cannot catch the meaning on the second or third bounce, I too become a mumbler. When the speaker says what sounds like "The trains in spades are ghostly in the rains," I answer, "Mmm" or if I wish to show enthusiasm, "McGooey." Both expressions seem to suffice. The last mumbler I talked to rambled on for 20 minutes. I got through that with 14 "Mmms" and 2 "McGooeys." I can't remember what the other party said, but I can recall every word I spoke. I must have a photographic memory.

Volume is another consideration. You might ask how you are coming through. Once in a while you can be too loud, but the too soft voice is more common. If you are paying long distance charges, and the other party can't hear you, you aren't getting your money's worth. At best you are wasting your and your listener's time.

Courtesy Comes First

Far and away the most important consideration, however, is to make sure all callers are treated with total
courtesy. Don't be "lippy," and don't allow your people to be.
With someone you know, maybe; but never be flippant with
a stranger.

I remember with great clarity a conversation I had
almost fifteen years ago. I had called the home office of a
national food products company and said, "They told me to
call this number."

The person on the other end sneered, "And who are
'they'?"

Even though my opening remark was admittedly weak,
it certainly didn't warrant such a snide and deliberately
rude response. I eventually did learn the information I was
seeking, but the frustration of being treated rudely has
remained in my mind all these years. You don't want your
people to leave that kind of impression on your customers.

Creative Use of the Phone

Sometimes the phone will make contact for you when
nothing else can. And there's no denying that you can get
results right away. If you have to deal with two or more
widely separated individuals, you can even arrange a conference call. Of course try your best to get the real decision-
maker into the hookup.

Outside of bill collectors and your unemployed brother-
in-law, there are very few who will travel very far to meet
you. Unless you use the phone there is no way of getting
Jones of Toledo, Murphy of Boston, and Hanson of St. Louis
together without two of them doing some traveling—which
is not likely unless you foot the bill. (And if you can afford
that kind of expense money, the Drug Enforcement Agency
might decide to attend your sales meeting too!)

You probably will have more occasion to use the phone

to make appointments than for any other reason. Here the superstar comes to the fore because clients and their well-coached secretaries are crafty and may try to cut you off at the pass.

I usually tell a receptionist my name when I phone, but when I forget I do not like to hear: "May I say who is calling?" or worse yet, "Could you state the purpose of your call?"

A friend who makes big bucks through phoning, will oblige on the first question but not on the second. He handles both questions by this short statement: "This is ----. My number is ----. Please ask Ms. Jones to call me as soon as she's free."

Howard Chan, of the popular Ming Shee Café in Peoria, Illinois, uses another method. He answers both questions very quickly: "This is the IRS." He says it gets action right away.

One last quick one about Skinhead. When a local pest used the same IRS ploy, old Skinhead snapped back, "I thought you SOBs had forgotten me."

When you call ahead, don't actually state your business, but you can still be generous. Offer your client two options. Suggest a 1 P.M. meeting. If that is not satisfactory, offer a 9 A.M. appointment. The second option is usually acceptable if the first is not. Very few people are willing to admit they are not at their stores or offices by 9 A.M.

Calling ahead is just good sense. But let's suppose that after leaving Client A, you decide to have a go at walking in cold on Client B just down the hall.

In our world of meetings, the odds are you won't get to see your second client on a walk-in basis, but there you are. You ask the receptionist how long the meeting will last. The receptionist is just as much in the dark as you; you might as well ask for a weather prediction. So what do you do? That depends on your schedule. If your next appointment is something more certain, you might just as well leave your card and move on.

On the other hand, if you have a choice about staying or

leaving, up your odds by phoning your client right then and there. If the receptionist at Company B cannot direct you to a private phone, walk back to the place you just left down the hall. Tell the receptionist at Company A that you just remembered you need to make a call before you leave the building.

Then call your second client. The chances are, the receptionist at Company B won't recognize your voice, so be bold. When you are told that "Ms. Larson is in conference," see what you can do. Ask if you can be put through to the conference room. Maybe it cannot be done, but I have broken the sacred barriers to the inner sanctum. If you cannot get through, be philosophical: You lose some, you win some. Just keep on using ingenuity and determination. Your winnings will eventually top the average superstar's in the Super Bowl.

CHAPTER 7

The Centipede
Uses 100 Legs
to Get Ahead

In a way promotion and selling are the same thing. Promotion allows you to increase your reach. If you can contact the right buyers in large enough numbers, you can be a superstar. This fact should give you all the encouragement you need to forge ahead.

You might compare yourself to a centipede. The little insect has 100 legs—or so I am told; it can stub a couple dozen toes and still keep going. You also have a very large number of ways to get ahead.

For all I know the centipede doesn't need all its legs, but the legs are there to use when needed. You may not need all the following promotional suggestions, but you will need a number of them. In fact, you absolutely must have some of them. I am presenting these ideas as they come to mind. Some of these promotional ideas I am repeating from other parts of this book. That way you will have the most important revenue builders included in your centipede file. I am also including several items that are not—strictly speaking—promotional, but provide important pointers to keep in mind as you work on improving sales promotion.

1. *Mail.* I mean letters with a specific offer, with a self-addressed postcard and an expiration date. The minimum batch of 1,000 letters should normally be hand-addressed and must bear first-class postage. The postcards should be franked (that is, preprinted with a return permit that allows you to pay the postage when you receive the replies) but need not be hand-addressed.

2. *Yellow Pages.* Your business should be advertised with a display ad in the Yellow Pages, not just be listed. The ad can be as small as a column wide and two inches deep, or as large as a half-page. Include a picture of yourself in the ad.

You had better double or triple check your order. If your listing is fouled up in the Yellow Pages, it will be that way for an entire year. If you can, demand a proof of your ad. If your friendly phone company refuses to oblige, you may be able to find an independent directory. The *Northwest Minnesota Area Telephone Directory,* for example, describes itself as "an all-purpose directory" that "has no connection whatsoever with any telephone company."

If such a directory also refuses to provide you with a proof, you may be in the wrong business. There is a definite need for a directory that not only accurately lists and describes your business but also provides your zip code number. I'll take 100 shares if you go into production.

3. *Telephone.* You must have at least one phone that is answered 24 hours a day, 7 days a week. When I used an answering device I normally handled 100 additional calls a month, calls that otherwise could have been lost. When I

averaged 10 prospects out of 100 calls I could say I paid for the device the first week I used it.

Remember, an unguarded phone will ring, but your cash register won't.

4. *Shopper ads.* Those free newspapers with local ads and classifieds, mailed to everyone in a given area are called shoppers. For a bit extra you can buy an ad on the front page (which you usually can't do with regular newspapers), so if you want to be sure to make the front page, use shoppers. Their back pages are also high-drawing positions.

Some shoppers—the better ones, anyway—run news stories. If you have a newsworthy item, and can present it properly, you may get some free publicity. Of course you'll have to do all the work of writing the story, but it's good practice for writing crisp sales letters.

There are plenty of things to write about if you just stop to think. Let us say one of your salesmen is retiring or you have sold a vacant building. So you decide to write about the sale of the building to Radio Shack, which is opening a new store in the trade area of your neighborhood shopper.

The rawest cub reporter knows about the importance of a good lead sentence. If possible, it should answer the five W's: who, what, when, where, and why. For good measure the reporter will take care of "how" as well.

You will probably throw away enough paper to kindle the logs in your fireplace, but you stay at it. Finally, you come up with this opening sentence, your lead paragraph: "Radio Shack Inc., according to local realtor Laura Smith, Tuesday purchased the recently vacated Farmer's Bank building here." You could have added that the building will be used as a retail outlet, but that would add length to your sentence, thus reducing the punch of your statement. Besides, Radio Shack is nationally known as a retailer.

The rest of your news item should present other details that you and the buyer are prepared to release; the price, the name of the official who represented the company, when the new store will open, how long the building stood vacant.

Use the most interesting facts first. The weakest statement ordinarily should come at the end. If you have written more paragraphs than the editor can use, it is easy to chop off one or more at the end of the story.

Even shoppers have a time frame, so plan your news item to be usable either soon before or soon after the event. And make sure you present it professionally. Don't dream of handwriting your piece. Type it on good paper, double spaced with decent margins: two inches at the top, one and a half inches at the left, one inch at the right, and a solid inch at the bottom of each page. Better yet, if you can obtain what news people call "copy paper," use it. It is easy for editors to handle, and it suggests to the editor that you know at least something about the newspaper business. It will prejudice her in your favor enough to get her to read the first sentence.

Days, even weeks later, some of your more observant clients may remember your news item: "Hey, you're the one who got someone into that vacant bank. Good show. Town needs some life."

5. *Lunch*. I can hold my weight on two light meals a day, but I like to eat lunch with prospects or clients even if I have to skimp on breakfast and supper. I find it actually costs more to eat at my desk or to go home at noon.

There is a joke among my clients about eating with me in the Minneapolis Radisson Hotel: "It costs you $1,000 to sit at Sheehan's table at the Radisson Grill." I'd been going there for 25 years, so the waiter always reserved my table. When a customer sat down with me, my waiter gave me a knowing wink; he knew he would get a better tip when I closed a deal.

Normally my guest and I would just sit and talk. I did not use high-power sales tactics. I enjoyed the get-togethers even when I did not close. When you give, you always get something in return, even if it's only a relaxing break in your day.

6. *Gifts*. Novelty items and small gifts are usually given out around Christmas by merchants, bankers, sales-

people, and anyone else who wants to make an impression. Other sellers all over the nation make husky incomes just selling these items. Gifts of this kind must be productive, otherwise they would not sell so well.

7. *Classified Ads.* Small ads in the classified section of newspapers, shoppers, or magazines can be very effective in hard times. Be sure to list the item, the price, your phone number, and your name.

8. *Handbills.* Flyers can be effective, in minimum distributions of 1,000 copies. However, be careful: some motorists are not happy with handbills stuck under their windshield wipers.

Some delivery people also are not happy about all the walking they have to do. Back in my youth I knew of carriers who simply dumped the handbills down the sewer. Nowadays the process is often reversed. The sewer is poured into the handbills.

9. *Newspaper Ads.* There are small businesses all over the country that survive on matchbook-sized ads. If you want to find out how effective these small ads are, you might call the sponsoring person or company. Explain that you are not a competitor but would like to get some information for your own projects. Of course, regular display advertising in both dailies and weeklies is usually larger in size and changed more frequently. The wheels of industry would almost stop without this help.

Sometimes it is difficult to tell how effective your ads are, but if you can trace enough business to your use of the newspapers, you had best keep at it. Your own name or the name of your firm must always be in the public eye. The larger the area, the easier it is for you to drown in a sea of indifference.

I would suggest you always mention an approximate price for more expensive items. If you say "under $300 for a fireplace insert," you may get people curious enough to call.

10. *Bank Displays.* Are you audacious enough to ask the president of your bank if you can set up a display of your books, photos of homes and estates, or a miniature mobile

home? At Richfield State Bank (Minnesota) I saw a realtor standing beside an easel holding blow-ups of development sites. Observers could take a calling card out of a large box if they were interested. This continued for a month, and people continued to pick up the cards.

If the banker treats you like the seeker of an unsecured loan, offer to display samples of *his* goods in *your* window.

11. *Fairs and other events.* Every store owner depends on walk-in business. What better can you ask for than a county or state fair where prospects by the thousands have already walked in? People who would never stop in your store will stand and watch your movie or demonstration, or take one of your free fortune cookies. You smile at folks as they pick up your cookies. They smile as they read the enclosed message: "Confucius say, 'Person who walk into beehive get stung. Whoever walk into Decorators Furniture get treated like mandarin.' "

A number of communities sponsor celebrations such as Pioneer Days or Crazy Days. These promotions give merchants a chance to unload slow-moving merchandise. Just a bridge table or picnic table in front of your store is about all that is required. You can embellish the setup with odd costumes or decorations, anything that will catch the eye..

Nice summer days are great for this kind of promotion, but did you folks who live in the snow belt ever think of trying it in the winter? I do not know of anyone who has tried it. I do not know of anyone who used the telephone, either, before Bell invented it.

12. *Displays.* You can set up displays on front lawns, sidewalks, windows, air terminals. But wherever you set up a display make everything attractive, especially the prices.

I spent my first five years in business with Colgate Palmolive, traveling the country selling Palmolive soap, Cashmere Bouquet, Ajax Cleanser, Fab, Crystal White, and Honeysuckle. Invariably my customers expected me to help them display and sell my products. I didn't mind doing it. If they could not move the merchandise, I got no repeat orders.

When you set up displays in your customers' stores, you teach them your ideas about merchandising. If they use your display techniques, they will sell more of your product. Of course they may also wind up selling your competitor's products. Forget your competitor. It is your customers you care about.

Your windows and other displays should be changed every week. Don't give folks a chance to take your window for granted.

But if you are short of capable hands to dress up your window, you should try to find a more enduring display. A growing plant might do the trick, especially if you offer a substantial prize for guessing the plant's weekly or monthly growth. There is a prize in it for you too: a lot of extra business.

One establishment I like to frequent is Wags Restaurant on Highway 1 at Cutler Ridge, Florida. They display a complete meal in their lobby. The display, protected by a small plexiglass dome, is mostly real food and is changed every day.

I have eaten their giant sausages on two occasions after seeing them displayed in the lobby. Considering that I am a very determined dieter, you would have to say that Wag's display has pulling power. The next time I'm there I think I'll suggest a separate entrance for dieters.

If it is your own store, do not forget that the whole place is a display. It should be sparkly clean. Doors and windows should be washed every day. Clean floors are a must. I once asked my wife why she never dropped into a store that I knew had good products at proper prices. She is a very astute shopper so I was surprised she did not try it. Her reason was simple: "The place looks dirty."

Employees at the well-known White Castle hamburger places clean when they are not busy. A couple of years ago Phyllis and I stayed at the famed Fontainebleau in Miami.

When the staff people were not actually serving guests, they were cleaning and making certain everything was shipshape.

Your office may be your only showplace. If so, make sure it's in good order. If you are at work, there is a kind of "active clutter" that callers expect. Debris that is too old and too deep is another thing. A cluttered, messy desk smells of unfinished business. A client could easily suspect that his business will join the debris.

A current cute saying would have us believe that clutter is all right: "An empty desk is the sign of an empty mind." To that I have two answers:

1. The full mind signified by clutter is sadly disorganized and its owner is a chronic procrastinator.

2. The person with a cluttered desk is the lady or gentleman who spends an extra half hour a day looking for lost contracts, titles, car keys, credit cards, and appointments.

13. *Trade Shows.* Conventions, boat shows, home and garden shows, sport shows—these are all good crowd pullers. Usually, exhibiting at these functions is expensive, but they are the places where you may find your kind of buyer. If you are selling sports clothing, the sport show could be your answer. If you are pushing high fashion, you have to look elsewhere.

"Dutch" Ackermann and his charming wife, Billie Jo, owners of a popular fishing lodge in Ontario that draws customers from all over the United States, believe strongly in trade shows. Even though a lot of their business is from repeat customers, they still sponsor booths at sport shows in Dallas, Chicago, and Minneapolis. Billie and Dutch would sooner skip their own vacation than miss these sport shows. To keep people coming to a camp that charges $150.00 a day you cannot afford to miss on your promotional efforts.

I was given a live demonstration of the effectiveness of trade shows when I attended the 15th Annual Miami International Travel Camping Show. I rode up to the exhibition with my friends Helen and Gregor Weiland in their 1970 model motor home.

There were literally acres of travel vehicles in the parking lot. The show was well attended by confirmed recreational-vehicle users who had paid $3.50 admission, so they were not idle spectators.

My feet are like New Year resolutions; they give out easily. So while the Weilands studied the magnificent residential chariots I found a comfortable chair in a shady spot. A sales representative for BeachCraft Motorhomes, joined me at the same table. He also needed a soft spot after seven hours down and four to go.

The rep had already attended shows in Louisville, Kentucky, the country's largest; Elkhart, Indiana; Lehigh Valley, Pennsylvania; and Sarasota and Fort Meyers, Florida. Other shows are held in San Antonio, Dallas, Pittsburgh, Minneapolis, and many other places. With all that work I figured he had to be accomplishing something. "Yes," he assured me. "Shows such as this are the best place to sell recreational vehicles, and the last two days are the best."

Another seller had joined us. He added, "I sold four units the first day. The rigs were all in the $30,000 range."

While we talked I was sitting in a Barth Model '84 motor home priced at $181,000. My friend Gregor was on the outside looking it over. The superseller told me that just by selling the unit I was loafing in, his company could justify the cost of participation in the show: $5,000 for a three-unit space plus $1,000 a week in expenses. Some companies will split the cost of a show with retailers. Most will share expenses. A few dummies say: "No dice."

I would have gathered a lot more information, but just then Gregor came inside and asked for a demonstration. The superseller, like many other exhibitors, kept a "just in case" demonstrator in the parking area.

To round out this story it would be nice to say that we drove home in a new 35-foot motor home. It would be nice, but not quite true. We drove home in Gregor's old 1970 model.

When Helen, Gregor, and their guests, waved goodbye at my place in Homestead, Florida, a few days later, they were still using the 1970 motor home. However, they were in a bit of a hurry. A superseller was waiting at Sarasota to close the sale on their new travel home, and close it he did.

14. *Mail-O-Grams.* These eye-catching mailing pieces can be very effective when they tell of something new or a special offer. I just received a "Thank-U-Gram" from a Firestone service center. It was much appreciated.

15. *Billboards.* Only one percent of the advertising dollar goes for outdoor signs in this country, yet they can be very effective. With proper lighting, your billboard gives you 24-hour service. You can be certain that travelers will welcome signs telling them the location and prices of eateries, gas stations, and motels.

I disagree with Lady Bird Johnson. Some signs provide a real service. When my gas gauge registers near the empty mark, I would rather see a gas sign than the Garden of Eden.

16. *Your Picture.* Get your portrait on everything you possibly can: ads, calling cards, billboards, matchbooks, postcards, church and lodge bulletins. People eventually start to recognize you. Even if you are not beautiful or handsome, folks get used to your appearance. You won't scare them off when they see you face to face.

Fred Russell of Boulder, Colorado, used his picture in every ad he placed in newspapers, and he doubled his business in a year. A Minneapolis businessman put his picture in church bulletins and got aboaut 12 orders a year. Even if you are mad at your minister, you cannot pass up an opportunity like that.

17. *Co-op Advertising.* Manufacturers often have co-op advertising dollars for their distributors. You can use these allowances for displays, radio, newspapers, TV, etc.

You can save money sometimes by teaming up with others who sell the same product but do not compete. This way you can afford more expensive media such as TV, magazines, and metropolitan dailies.

18. *Radio.* You will find that radio can do some things that no other media can. You can listen to the radio while you're driving, waking up in the morning, or trying to sleep at night.

Radio advertising must be long-term; just one or two ads won't do it. If you are sure you can make it pay, get into it, and stay with it. A Minnesota car dealer has been running a remote broadcast for 13 years. As far as I know, it is the oldest advertising program of its kind in the nation. Every Saturday the broadcast sells cars with the on-the-scene aid of pop, sandwiches, popcorn, and other free goodies.

A broadcaster once told me that the average comprehension of radio listeners was at the level of a 12-year-old. At any rate you must consider whom you want to reach. If you are selling skateboards, surfing equipment, hit records, and mod clothing, you may make a killing on a rock station. Country-western music gets very heavy listenership in some areas. To sell luxury cars, expensive homes, yachts, planes, and fine electronics equipment, you should consider a station that features semi-classical or classical music.

19. *Store Contests.* Contests can be a terrific way to build traffic. Almost everyone wants something for nothing, even if they have to come into your store to get it.

Not long ago a store in my area mailed out keys that were to be brought into the store and used to try to unlock a treasure chest. I remember buying a few things while waiting my turn to try my key in the chest.

In the Winn Dixie stores a free bingo game is popular right now. Each purchaser get a small lift-off paper tab with a concealed number. One of the classic store games was the bean-guessing contest. You do not see it much any more, but it set many a tongue wagging about the big jar of beans in Murphy's Grocery.

An expensive but attention-getting stunt is the shopping contest. Entrants try to fill their carts with the most expensive load of groceries. In many cases such contests even win you some free publicity.

20. *Private Sales.* Your preferred customers not only like special treatment, they deserve it. All you have to do is give them a special incentive at a special time.

Lowell Anderson recently packed his store, Furniture Studios, in Cambridge, Minnesota, with customers at an off-hours time. He just mailed a postcard to his best customers. Previously he had tried expensive stationery, but it did not attract customers as well as the postcards. He was literally swamped with customers at the time set for the special sale.

An invitation to a meal will bring its reward. Even coffee and donuts will bring people to your bank or store, but you could try something more imaginative. I once served a noon luncheon to a crowd of 200 persons with just two people helping. The main course, fish chowder, was embellished with crackers, croutons, and coffee and ice cream bars for dessert. Many came back for seconds, and many compliments were paid the cook. What I liked most, though, was the grocery bill: only $83.72.

21. *Coupons.* Coupons that offer 10, 15, or 20 percent discounts will bring people into your store. To speed up the action set an expiration date, or take a tip from many television advertisers and add the warning, "But act now, this offer is limited." The sponsors may be still saying the same thing a year from now, but they are not really lying. What they are implying is, "This offer is limited to the time it takes to run out of customers."

Clipping coupons is a morning ritual in many households. We are all familiar with newspaper and magazine coupons, but there are other types. I received a 50-cent coupon when I paid my check at Nelson's café in Minneapolis. It would have brought me back for breakfast the next day, but I had an appointment at another place.

Bob Hendrickson used a wooden nickel at Windy Corner, a beer tavern he operated in Euclid, Minnesota. If someone wanted to buy a round before all the glasses were empty, the bartender passed out wooden nickels to those slackers who were stalling on their drinking. Some even took the nickels home or carried them around until they got thirsty. The little pine coupons could easily have been adopted as legal tender in Euclid, but the temperance people would not accept the wooden nickels. Neither would the IRS.

22. *Referrals*. My best guess is that 20 percent of all goods and services are sold in America on a referral basis. Until recently all doctors and lawyers secured clients in that fashion. In the housing industry, one out of five houses was sold through referrals. To help secure these positive referrals, do your utmost to make certain your customers have only the best to say of you.

23. *Customer Assistance*. This promotion is based on the same thing as referrals; your reputation as an honest, competent merchandiser. If you leave a customer with a taste of rejected Limburger cheese, forget about this promotion.

A customer who is not only satisfied but is enthusiastic about your product may even go with you to call on a prospect. Restaurants are among the most frequent beneficiaries of this kind of help. I have taken scores of friends to an Italian café near the University of Minnesota in Minneapolis. Many of my friends went back again with more friends.

I convinced the Chamber of Commerce in North St. Paul, Minnesota, to take my sales course by bringing a satisfied student to the Chamber office. My student declared, "He was the first guy that ever taught me how to close." The Chamber enrolled 28 people in my class.

24. *Professional Help*. Advertising agents may be expensive, but they are very imaginative people. Even if you cannot afford a professional advertising agent or public relations counselor, you may still do all right. If you can find a friend or anyone else who likes to promote things, you may have stumbled on a gold mine. Is there someone who manages an annual community affair? She or he may be looking for new worlds to conquer. Just ask your local promoter if she or he would like to earn some extra money. You could offer a fixed sum for every idea that you feel you

can use. You could even offer a commission on the extra business.

Promotional people are often "hams" who will do almost anything to get into the limelight. If you can provide some real or would-be promoter with an audience, you will have just the idea-mill you need.

25. *News.* You could be doing something newsworthy this very day. Small newspapers, radio stations, or TV stations are always in need of news. If you are doing something unusual—staging a promotional breakfast, introducing a new product, expanding your sales force—you have something of news value. If you can speak on your feet you might even be interviewed.

You will be happily surprised at how helpful reporters and news directors can be if you approach them as you would one of your clients. Too many people look down on communicators who are not in the so-called "big time." If you think, as so many do, that you can do a better job than they can, just try to write a news article that compares with an item in your daily paper.

Before you start any serious news writing, read a good book on news preparation. You will find that the style for radio and newspapers is different. I would say it is easier to write for the airwaves.

Look back at number 4 in this chapter, where we talked about writing news releases for shoppers. The same rules apply for local weekly or daily papers.

You would use basically the same approach to get some favorable radio publicity. Let's look at the same example, selling the old bank building to Radio Shack. As a starter, why not line up a Radio Shack executive to be interviewed on one of the local radio station's talk shows or news broadcasts? In the process of setting up an interview, you will also get to know the news director and the announcer. Then the next time you have an idea to promote, your contact will be that much easier.

Using a newspaper story to spin off into a radio interview is just one example of the superstar's ability to get one thing to lead to another and another. It is what you might call "imagineering": using your imagination to get more out of your mental, physical, moral, and financial resources.

Whatever you do, make sure that all the media get your release. You may be concerned only with radio listeners, but if your news item is really worthwhile the TV station and the local newspaper will be interested as well. In fact the editor of the paper and the news director of the TV station may remember you unfavorably if you slight them.

Very few take advantage of available publicity. Those who do are in the abode of the superstar. Invite yourself in by learning to use publicity to progress in your field. Probably the best available book to guide you to success with the media is *The Publicity Handbook* by David R. Yale, (Bantam Books, New York).

26. *Clubs.* Business and fraternal groups can be a big help to you. However, they may not help you enough to justify joining for business reasons alone. If you enjoy the sociability of meeting new people and getting new ideas, groups like the Rotarians, Lions, Kiwanis, or Optimists will serve you well.

27. *Higher Profit Items.* Without selling to the Pentagon you can still make higher profits on certain items. This is where your research and imagination will pay dividends.

A touch of class—every superstar should have it—can make the difference between "No Sale" and a laughter-filled trip to the bank. I learned this truth on a trip to Sun Valley way back in the 1940s.

A general store in the nearby town of Ketchum, Idaho, had been trying to sell a batch of broad-brimmed straw hats, the kind you wear in the garden. The price was only $3 or $4, but there were scarcely any buyers. The store owner was as distressed as the merchandise. When a posh shop at Sun Valley offered him $2 a hat, the grateful merchant almost licked the buyer's hand.

The hats quickly went on display in the second shop at $20 each. Thrilled ski bunnies from all over the country bought the hats in a matter of days, and hurried home to brag about their bargains.

28. *Unique Merchandise.* As we all know, if you build a better mousetrap the world will beat a path to your door. It's human nature to look for something better. Not everyone finds it, but we all keep looking.

Antiques, fine art, rare coins, and many other items are very salable if you can find the right buyer. In fact, a connoisseur of classic cars would buy a Pierce Arrow in mint condition quicker than an ordinary buyer would make a loan payment on a subcompact.

29. *Fill in the Holes.* Your competitors have weaknesses. So do you. You search for both, but you act differently when you find them. Your weaknesses you correct. Your competitors' you convert to your own strength.

If Joe Blow's clerks look more appropriate on Halloween than they do during the rest of the year, don't tell Blow about it. Joe will not believe you anyway. If he does, he won't do anything about it. But you can profit from his mistakes.

Capitalizing on another's weakness is another way of improving your presence. If you are selling sports cars you will surely want your salespersons to wear something more free and easy than a frown. We usually associate a sports car with a breezy, happy spirit. Smile. Teach your staff to smile. Anyone who won't smile should be traded off to Joe Blow.

30. *Research.* It is quite obvious that reading sales or self-help books is important, but it is also important to be well-informed on other matters.

Your local library can provide you with information that no other source could supply. In a new territory you will be better prepared for the art of selling if you know something about its makeup. Read the history of the area. Learn about its people, business, climate, and employment conditions. Learn anything you can that will help you deal with and talk with your clients.

31. *Travel.* Travel broadens more than your hips. Your

horizons are made wider and your insights deeper. Someday someone who has traveled to Russia is going back there and sell them on a better method of constructing their buildings and bridges. One day Phyllis and I are going to Japan and China to see what is going on and to relax our minds.

32. *Sports.* Columnist Sidney Harris says that while religion was once called the opiate of the people, sports now holds that title.

Testimonials from well-known sports stars are a sure-fire promotion, if you can afford it. If you don't have that kind of budget, consider sponsoring a sport. Thousands of bowlers, softball players, and other sports participants get a lot of good recreation through sponsored sports. Since the players have a lot of relatives and friends you are also likely to get some benefit.

Bob Hoskins, now living in Emporia, Kansas, used to own and operate two delicatessens in Tennessee. At the same time he sponsored a semi-pro baseball club that cut a fine figure in the lesser leagues. It must have been successful. Years ago he received an offer for both enterprises, the kind he could not refuse.

33. *Spot Checking.* Perhaps this is another form of research. If so, it is a good one. Select five or six advertisements from papers out of your territory. Write or call the sponsors of the ads. Explain that you are in the same business and would like to exchange some ideas about advertising, particularly the insertions that caught your eye.

Your new contacts may even like the idea of placing some cooperative ads with you. More advertising dollars may enable you and your new pen-pals to try some more expensive advertising: magazines, area radio, and TV.

34. *Specials.* Specials bring people to your store or showroom. They also help clear out merchandise that is not moving. The prices do not have to be the only things that are special. Specials can be for special people: senior citizens, PTA members, homecoming guests, Girl and Boy

Scouts, graduates. The list is as long as your imagination.

Weekly, monthly, or annual specials work well for food, furniture, cars, and many other items. Be careful not to put everything "on special;" then the sale items would cease to be special.

Another important thought about specials: it is better to have someone else carry out the merchandise than to do it yourself—or worse yet, have a distress broker do it.

35. *Family Shopping*. Children are often nuisances, but I like nuisances that talk their parents into buying candy and ice cream. If you are building a future for your place of business you will do well to cater to younger people. You might even consider a special playroom for them. Kids remember.

Kids will also remember the bad things. As a teenager I was addicted to fishing, and often shopped for fish baits. On one occasion, the only clerk in the store was busy in the back room. When he saw me at the fishing lure counter he yelled, "Don't be loafing around here, kid." Then he thought better of his remark and added, "Or were you looking for something?"

I was loaded with cash—95 cents—so I was a bit bold: "I was, but not anymore." Actually, I was saving face. The lure I wanted was 98 cents; way over my reach.

Children are eager consumer. Though they lack discretionary income, they do have parents. Gearing your business toward family shopping can be profitable.

36. *Check the West*. Fads used to start in the East. Now they start in the West and spread across the country. Surely many businesses would like to know these fads ahead of time.

Here is an opportunity to use travel to your own benefit. Check with your tax preparer. You may be able to deduct the trip. I would bet my appetite that a superstar would find a way to tame the IRS. When you get back from your trip, assemble your findings for publication. Send out sample copies of a newsletter to businesses that could use the information. I would call it *Western Trends*, or *Future*

Markets, or possibly *Coming Changes*. Mail out your initial copies with a letter explaining what you are doing, but be sure to enclose a franked return envelope.

What should you charge? You should add up your trip costs plus your printing (mimeographing?) and mailing costs, and divide by the number of expected returns. An acceptable mail reply is two percent, so you could expect two subscribers for every 100 mailing pieces. Now let us assume your trip West cost $1,500, and your first mailing of 10,000 pieces cost $2,000 for postage and $500 for labor and materials. Divide your total cost of $4,000 by 200, your expected rate of return. Your subscription charge could be $20. That is your breakeven figure, and quite low for a newsletter. To be fair with the IRS, you should aim for a profit. If you win they win. If you lose they lose.

My humble suggestion is that you make your subscription fee $30 and offer a $5 introductory discount for cash with the order. Those whom you have to tempt with a second mailing should pay the full rate.

Please put me on your mailing list. I'll subscribe to the first "trends" newsletter offer I receive.

37. *Style Show*. Dress shops, of course, often use shows as promotions, but others can use them effectively too. A Wisconsin dealer in storage facilities staged a fashion show for the wives of all the farmers who bought silos during the year. Attendance at the show was SRO—standing room only. You can be certain that few husbands bought silos from the competitor.

38. *Appreciation Fetes*. Steak dinners with champagne were served at an appreciation night in Portage, Wisconsin, recently. The sponsors made no sales pitches; they just thanked their guests for their business.

In Progresso, Mexico, just across the Rio Grande from southern Texas, the whole city declares an annual appreciation day for American business. The crowds are wined, dined, and royally entertained. The happy crowd more than doubled the town's population the day I attended the festival. The multitudes of overwhelmed Americans returned the appreciation with a shower of "green" on the Progresso shops and cantinas.

39. *The Chamber of Commerce.* If you are the operator of a business, you probably are already a member, but other sellers should consider joining also. Remember, you are a citizen of your town. Give a hand with Chamber activities; it will help you get acquainted.

40. *Name Tags.* If you are like me you appreciate name tags. I once forgot my own birthday; imagine what I can do with a name.

In your store your tag should identify you and your position. Even other salespersons who call will appreciate knowing whether they are addressing the manager or the janitor. Don't be alarmed if someone reads your tag and calls you by your first name. If someone calls you "muttonhead" and buys, you are better off than if your customer called you "madam" or "sir" and only asked for the bathroom.

41. *Newsletters.* In addition to suggestion 37, you can easily put together a newsletter for your own establishment or personal sales effort.

For this type of letter you cannot, of course, charge a fee—or can you? (My gas company charges me to reconnect my fuel supply when I return to Florida for the winter so I can be sold more gas.)

You could try to charge for your newsletter; but, on second thought, you probably could not get away with it. After all, you are not a public utility. If you are, you do not need this book. All you need is the legislators.

To set up your own newsletter about all you need is a good method of duplicating your material. Billie Jo Ackermann uses her IBM memory typewriter to send out from 600 to 1,000 letters about the fishing at Caribou Falls Lodge in Ontario. Each letter is personalized with the correct name of the addressee in the salutation. Most of her promotional letters go out from the Ackermann home in Dallas, but she somehow manages to get some out during their very hectic camping season.

You may find that mimeographing or copier duplicating will fit your needs. If it works, you can cut down from first-class to permit mail, quite a saving. You can even staple in the reply card or envelope, the all-important essential of practically every mailing piece.

What you put into your newsletter is up to your ingenuity. You may even wander from the subject of your product or service, but whatever you write about should be interesting. Minkota Power Cooperative, based in Warren, Minnesota publishes a monthly newsletter that includes a column on fishing. "The Sabaskong Angler" features fishing news about Lake of the Woods, winter and summer.

One-person sales staffs do not ordinarily attempt newsletters, but who is talking about something ordinary? We are looking at superstars. We are examining people who make the unusual usual. The extraordinary is their way of life.

To help you crank your duplicator to new sales records, you should consider subscribing to *The Ragan Report*, 407 S. Dearborn St., Chicago, IL 60605, phone (312) 922-8245. It will probably cost about $80 a year, but it's the only source I know of that keeps you up to date on business communications.

42. *Mailing Lists.* A good card file of your current and former customers plus a listing of your prospects is a must. You should work at it daily if possible. If you let address changes go too long, your client may have moved again.

Color coding your files according to your needs will save you hours of tedious work. If you have a photographic memory you might dispense with a file, but in that case you probably wouldn't be selling anyway; you'd be appearing on quiz shows.

43. *Dress.* Your attire should reflect success. You want to inspire confidence. If you use too much makeup or wear a garish tie, your client may suspect that you are really in another kind of work.

I know of one bearded insurance agent who sold a million dollars' worth of policies every year. Yet I would not recommend a beard or mustache. I have found that male lip adornments are resented about 80 percent of the time.

44. *Twenty-Four Hour Sales.* In larger cities this promotion can bring you extra sales. People who would not dream of working after 5 P.M. will sit up half the night playing poker or bridge. To do the same thing for your sales record should be equally attractive.

If you are a lone star salesperson, you obviously cannot keep going 24 hours on your own, but you can come close once in a while. The country doctor usually established his practice by being available day or night. If you have a newsletter you might promote a day or night "sellathon." Ask your prospects to set the time, then be there. The next day you can catch up on your sleep with dreams of profits and bonuses dancing in your head.

45. *Sales.* I cannot believe I am at number 45 and haven't mentioned "just plain sales." Would you believe that you may never have to stage a sale if you use enough of the other promotions and use them well? Did you ever hear of a bank sponsoring a sale?

46. *Record Your Victories.* Each promotional effort that is successful should be written on your personal score sheet. You will not be able to forget your failures, but record them anyway. If you cannot make a given promotion work for you after honest efforts, you should try something else.

47. *Compete Only with Yourself.* Newspaper columnist Sidney Harris says that all great people have one common characteristic: they do not compare themselves with others, "but are content to run their own race on their own terms."

At this point you may be wondering: "Hey, you started out talking about the 100 legs of a centipede, so where are the other some-50 promotions?" Ah, check back. I never promised 100 promotions. However, if you wish to add to the list, feel free.

We may have produced a centipede with less than a hundred legs, but you cannot say we left you without a leg to stand on.

★★★★★★★★★ **CHAPTER 8** ★★★★★★★★★

Filling
Up the
Glasses

In the last chapter I gave you some of the promotional ideas I have seen used successfully over the years. If you try some of these techniques, and do them well, I can practically guarantee you'll have new customers flocking in.

But unless you give something of value, and treat them with plenty of care, they probably won't come back a second time. It is actually possible to promote yourself right out of business unless you provide an equal amount of attention to customer satisfaction.

There's a story about a barmaid who was less than generous in filling beer mugs. One day a customer told her that she could easily sell twice as much beer.

"How?" she demanded.

"Easy," said the customer. "Fill up the glasses."

I don't know if this actually happened, but I do know the principle is sound. It isn't in any of the sales manuals but if all businesses followed this slogan, there would be a lot fewer business failures.

Filling up the glasses has always been the straightest road to pleasing people. It will work for you. When glasses are filled up, you double much more than volume. You also increase customer confidence and loyalty. Your customers often become your best promoters. They advertise your business and pay for the privilege.

The Number One Sales Rule

This simple formula—"fill up the glasses"—works whether you have a sidewalk lemonade stand or a nationwide chain of restaurants, a one-person home repair business or a giant corporation. It's particularly important in those instances where one satisfied customer represents a very large sum. If you are hoping to make big ticket sales, you must be even more conscious of keeping your customers happy. If you help to keep your fat-cat buyer nice and plump, you'll usually be greeted with a friendly purr.

Here's another good reason for working hard to hold on to your big customers: it's cheaper. The average industrial sales call will cost you or your company up to $150. If you make five calls a day, that's a selling cost of $750 a day, or—brace yourself—about $15,000 a month.

No matter what type of selling is involved, you or your sponsor will have a lot of money invested in every customer you secure. So you cannot afford to be lazy. Some you just cannot hold. You can do practically nothing about companies that are taken over, go broke, or undergo drastic management changes. Yet what you sell, or do, or say can do a lot to keep those reorders coming. This is especially true if you are basically selling what you produce yourself.

Some super sellers do things to hold on to their bread-and-butter accounts that may seem unnecessary, even outlandish. I once met a superstar seller who was known as the "Fishing Salesman." His specialty was rolling-mill machinery: an item needed by only the largest foundries and steel processors. He was highly successful. His method? He worked on the folks who could do him the most good: shop foremen. He knew that when the need arose to replace machinery, the folks in high places would be steered to the right company.

His way of filling up the glasses was to take people fishing. His fishing bill alone came to $650 a week per person at a fly-in fishing paradise on God's Lake, Manitoba. According to the resort owner, the Fishing Salesman spent close to $25,000 a summer. He did this year after year, but he never complained. After all, he was filling his own glass at the same time.

This sort of extravagant treatment is even easier for multinational companies, such as the giant manufacturer that maintains a motor yacht on a Canadian lake. The boat and its crew of seven have just one purpose: to entertain the executives of only one company. This company is the only customer the manufacturer has for one of its products, and it had to sell just one of them to the company whose key people get a week of fishing on one of Canada's best fishing lakes. I almost forgot. The staff of the yacht includes a trained bartender, lest the executives forget who is filling their glasses.

Two Famous Fill-er-uppers

Sears, among for-profit companies, and the Mayo Clinic among the nonprofits are tops, I think, for their ability to fill up the glasses.

Sears' product responsibility is so strong that its clerks can skip their annual baths without scaring away the customers. The parent organization always stands behind what the stores sell. Of course, if I am equidistant from two Sears stores I will make a point of going to the one whose clerks are humanoid.

Among many retailers from whom I sought product adjustment, Sears stands out in gold, embossed letters. Their clerks can yawn in my face. I will still go back.

About ten years ago I bought a small calculator for about $110. It worked fine, but after I had it for about a year I left it turned on over the weekend. I could also smell the faint odor of burned wiring. I tried to add two and two and got zero.

Sheepishly I brought it back to the small Sears store where I had bought it. I explained exactly what had happened. I even resisted the temptation to blame it on my secretary. I left instructions to fix it if not too costly, or throw it away.

In a week I stopped at Sears to pick up my gadget. It was brand new, and there was no charge. Nine years later, the second calculator is still rolling merrily along.

My experience with Mayo Clinic, though of a different nature, was such that I can only sing their praises—off key, of course, but I sing when I think of them. Their collection policies are so painless as to be unreal. Almost ten years ago I left the clinic office owing $1,300. The accounting department asked me if $50 a month would be too much. I couldn't have been more happily surprised if the IRS had offered to lend me martini money.

Long after my bill was paid, the clinic regularly called me long distance to check on my condition. They finally quit calling about a year ago. I guess they got tired of my answer: "Healthy as a horse."

Success on a Smaller Scale

In your own way you can do what Sears and Mayo have done. It's amazingly simple: do the very best job you can.

I have one more example of a business that understands

about filling the glasses. Near Homestead, Florida, there is a roadside stand that is patronized by people from all over the United States. It isn't really advertised, it's open only from December through April, and it's not centrally located. Yet Knaus Berry Farm is bulging with customers.

It is not even easy to find. Most of the road vendors in that area set up their stands on Highway 27. The Knaus stand is several miles west of the highway, and there are no signs on any connecting road. Even when you are on the right road and abreast of the stand, it is not easy to see. You could easily drive past, and you would if you weren't looking for it.

But each year thousands do find it. Tourists and locals search out the Knaus stand, drawn by the fame of their fabulous cinnamon rolls. The day I stopped by, the aroma of those heavenly rolls filled the little store, but you couldn't get near them. The line of customers reminded me of the queue at the ticket office before the big game.

I'm tempted to say the proprietors really know how to fill the glasses, but it would seem inappropriate here. The folks who run the stand are members of a very strict religious group which would probably frown on the purveyance of spirits.

Still, in a way, the fill up the glasses principle is at work. The Knauses could have made those oversized beauties a bit smaller and filled them with far fewer rich ingredients. They might have asked for more than $2.25 per half dozen. I'm sure they would still sell their rolls, but I doubt if their place would have become a tourist attraction if they hadn't decided, so to speak, to fill up the glasses.

Too Big to Care?

Usually monopolies aren't too concerned about filling up the glasses. That must be the reason behind my miserable experience with a Bell Telephone store a while back.

When I decided to buy my own instrument, I picked out

a lightweight model, with a "ringer control." A day or so later I left on a long trip.

When I returned I had a better chance to test my $72 acquisition. Though the cord had a tendency to pop out of its socket, I could call out reasonably well. When someone tried to get me, it was a different matter. The ring was so soft that I couldn't hear it from another room over the sneeze of a housefly. No problem. I would turn up the volume on the ringer control. But ringer control I could not find. A switch, yes, but nothing to raise or lower the volume of the ring.

But I took it back to the phone store to exchange what I thought was defective merchandise, the manager tested it. "Perfect," she said; "it rings all right."

I could hear it too. No fly in the building had a cold that day. I explained that I wanted it louder and would the manager please show me how to locate the ringer control.

She pointed to the on–off switch. I protested that a shutoff switch was not a control. She insisted that the term "ringer control" meant "on-and-off." Furthermore, she pointed to a few tiny specks on the phone and said, "We can't possibly take this back—it's soiled."

Now that the Bell system has been broken up, there are a lot of moans made by people who see their local rates getting sky high. This may be true for a while. Bell will still be a monopoly in some phases of its various operations, but it now has healthy competition in long distance service and in providing equipment.

I predict that though Bell did perform well in many ways in the past, it will get better as the new Bell companies learn that if they do not fill up the glasses, some other bartender will.

CHAPTER 9

Stewing Will Not Cook a Problem

Out of 100 people who die every year, 99 perish from anxieties and frustration, but only one from overwork. I heard an industrial psychiatrist tell this to an audience of 1,000 people in Stockford, Ontario, as part of a speech on stress. Managing stress, he said, is much the same as managing one's self. You must do three things: accept your situation as it is, learn to cope with problems, and be well grounded in the basics.

Apparently he practiced what he preached, for he was happily making the lecture circuit at the age of 72.

Family Comes First

If you are fighting with your spouse and children, take a long, hard look at yourself. Your first inclination is to blame them. You are certain everything would run smoothly again if only they would change.

Now is the time to step aside a bit. Take a stroll in the park, read a funny book, go soak your spirit in the quiet of your church. Remember, there are two parties to your problem: your family and you. Now ask yourself: "Is there anything at all that I can change?"

If you won't change, you are unfair in asking your spouse to change. You may think you don't need to change. If you think that way, you have the answer to the problem. To be a "know-it-all" is an extreme form of vanity, so let us hope that is not your problem. Whatever it is, it is time to take a positive step.

You may need help from your clergyman or a marriage counselor, but make the effort. It may be easier than you think. If you are drinking too much, using drugs, playing around, spending too much, not getting enough rest and exercise, or worrying too much, you do not need anyone to tell you what to do. I don't want you to end up like the man whose wife filed a missing persons report. When asked to describe her husband, she said, "Well, he's fat, short, bald, near-sighted, and he sniffles all the——oh hell, forget it."

Once you just start a positive program of self-correction you will feel better. You may fail a time or two, but you can do it. I have a good friend who has undergone two heart bypass procedures and two dry-ups from alcoholism. He's now 55, looks about 40, and has just retired from his position as president of one of the largest real estate and insurance agencies in western Ontario.

I have said it many a time: "It is better to manage yourself and be content than to direct the world's largest multinational corporation without achieving happiness." This truth was expressed far better by the source of all wisdom: "For what is a man profited, if he shall gain the whole world, and lose his own soul?"

I would suggest that even if things are going reasonably well, you take time out with your spouse and children to work out a five-year plan. You might make some interesting discoveries if you spend just five consecutive evenings with your family to think out your long-term plan. You may even want to carry it farther than five years. Your foreign travel, your retirement, your contribution to society, your children's school and career goals should all be considered.

We are all, as Robert Ringer pointed out in *Winning Through Intimidation,* picking our way through a jungle. We need a good compass bearing to carry us through to a proper destination. A life spent in aimless wandering is worse than being lost in the forest.

Your plan may require you to abandon old patterns and learn new ones. Just turning off the TV to work out your five-year plan may get you excited about a weekly family review or brainstorming session. Get up earlier, eat and drink less, exercise more, do more things for others—especially your spouse and children—read more, write more closing plans. If you find all this too difficult, try praying and worshipping more.

You can practice your customer relations right in your own home. Your spouse and children are most dear to you. If you owned all of Saudi Arabia, that would still be the case.

Three Elements of Stress Management

Stress saps anyone's energy and attitude. You need to reduce it or, if possible, eliminate it. Your problem may not be the family feud just outlined. It could just be that everything is conspiring to load you down to the breaking point. Life should not be that way, and it certainly need not be.

You can never sell to your real capacity if you carry a zoo on your back. If you remember that life is like a coin, you will do better. Living requires us to be aware of both the positive and the negative—the heads and the tails, so to speak.

The corrective measures suggested for a family problem may not work on every stress problem. Nevertheless, the elements are those suggested by our 72-year-old psychiatrist:

1. *Accept your situation.*
2. *Deal with things ("face the music").*
3. *Apply the basics.*

Leo Buscaglia, author of *Living, Loving & Learning,* asked a dying man of 85 what he would do if he could live his life over. On his deathbed, the octogenarian replied: "I would go barefoot from April through October. I would more often watch the sun rise and set. I would look at God's wonders and realize what a fantastic universe this is." The old gentleman also thought he would talk to children more, do silly things once in a while, observe nature, and learn the names of the birds. His main wish was that he had been more thankful. I believe this gentleman was talking about the most basic of the basics: live life to the fullest, every day.

An essential part of applying the basics is keeping your sense of humor. Laughter knocks out depression, discouragement, and even anger. Best of all, if you can learn to laugh at yourself, it knocks out haughtiness.

The great Irish comedian, Hal Roach of Jury's Cabaret in Dublin, says that we all need to laugh. Laughter draws us together. Even when Roach imparts conventional wisdom he gives it a wry twist: "Live every day as though it were your last, and one day you'll be right."

I like many other basics. Pay your bills even if you have to drive your car another year or go out to eat less often. Sometimes people who owe a lot of bills overeat or overdrink to forget their debts for a while. It is better to wipe out the debts to help you forget about the excess eating and drinking.

Some Common Causes of Stress

In my own 50 years of living I have decided that half the stress in America today is caused by the people we work with, the other half is caused by procrastination. (When asked what should be done about all the procrastination in his company, the manager said, "We'll put that one off until next week's meeting.")

Bernard Baruch, the great financier and advisor to presidents, has an answer for both problems. For dealing with difficult employees or associates Baruch tells us, "The normal condition of mankind is trouble." He is reminding us not to feel sorry for ourselves, but to accept things as they are. (Rule number 1 from our 72-year-old psychiatrist friend.) If your employees were easier to cope with, they probably could get a better job someplace else. One of them might even be your boss.

To cope with procrastination, Baruch notes that the person "who can master his time can master nearly everything."

Anger

Many stress problems are brought on by anger and its wake of hatred and vengeance. To make progress we have to get over yesterday. Yesterday is a cancelled check. Today and tomorrow make your cash flow. If you are still eating your own energy by dwelling on yesterday's affront to your dignity, get it out of your system. The only way you can do that is to forgive.

We can all learn a profound lesson from Pope John Paul II, who visited in prison the man who had tried to assassinate him. Forgiveness perhaps unburdens the forgiver even more than the one pardoned. In fact, in many cases the forgiven person does not even know or care about the pardon. Just taking the load off your back is a plus.

To stay on the happy and productive path to real stardom you may need to unburden yourself of many things besides animosity. Some of our habits are like bags of cement on each shoulder: smoking, heavy drinking, overeating, staying up too late, too much card playing, too many opinions based on too little knowledge, too much ignorance, too much self-indulgence, too much greed, and too much dishonesty and self-deception. If there is ever a time to eliminate the negative, it is at the moment you decide to put your life together. It is what you must do to become an authentic superstar.

Trouble

Trouble can be a cause of stress, but it can also help you learn how to manage future stress. Vaccines are usually made from the germs they are designed to prevent. Trouble can build the antibodies to fight future disruptions of your life.

We cannot give up in the face of trouble. Consider weight lifters, who deliberately take on trouble, so to speak. By increasing the strain on their muscles, they force their biceps to grow in size and strength. By grappling with your troubles in an honest and prolonged effort, you force yourself to grow in ability and stature. The next trouble will be easier to handle.

Change

Change is inevitable in our lives. We can either accept it or, better yet, deliberately cause it. We have to do one or the other. Resisting it will put us in the same predicament as the buggy-whip maker after the invention of the horseless carriage.

Most modern inventions bring about changes, and most are good changes. It is up to the people who use them to give inventions a good direction. The self-indulgent resist needed change because they are too lazy and too easy on themselves to go through the agony of developing new approaches or new skills.

Change is not always progress, but all of us need to change. Quite often the changes we need most are required by our own shortcomings such as laziness, ignorance, or stubbornness. When change makes you more unselfish, more tolerant, and less cocksure, it is a move in the right direction.

Risk

Fear of risk breeds more stress than it should. No one can hedge all the bets. Every day is another venture full of risks. The more we try to eliminate them entirely, the more we shoot ourselves in the feet—or elsewhere.

If you are self-employed you're in a high-risk business, but so are many employees of the corporate giants. Mergers, recessions, strikes, or poor management decisions can pull the rug on almost any seemingly secure position.

If your employer calls the right side of the coin, he may or may not share its extra winnings with you. If he loses, you stand a good chance of going down the drainpipe too. As a lone wolf you risk a lot, but you get all the winnings when things go right.

Actually, if you think about it the greatest risk of all is

to risk nothing, to just sit there and let life overwhelm you. This is what we have come to call burnout.

Burnout

Twenty-five percent of a class of mine in Wyoming, and more than half of a similar group in St. Paul, admitted to burnout.

Nobody really knows what burnout is, but folks go ahead and have it anyway. About as close as I can come to a definition is that it is a state of deep discouragement bordering on despair. It can be accompanied by the temptation to throw in the towel.

Burnout is probably what the financiers and investors felt who jumped out of skyscraper windows on Black Friday of the 1929 market crash. It could also be what hit Willie Loman at the end.

Why not have a "joyout" instead? Life goes on even if your selling slump is older than your car. You should not take yourself so seriously. I recall a statement so loaded with wisdom that it deserves to be displayed on the portico of every church, synagogue, and public building. I think it formed a tombstone epitaph:

> *The mills of the gods grind slowly,*
> *but they grind exceeding fine;*
>
> *Whom the gods would destroy they*
> *first make drunk with power;*
>
> *And if it becomes dark enough you*
> *can see the stars.*

Sometimes you just have to take time off—like when you cannot seem to get the corners of your mouth above chin level. Instead of bringing home the bacon, do something entirely different. When was the last time you found a sandy road and walked for an hour or two? Go with your spouse, take the kids, but go. Pick some wildflowers to share over the supper table.

I especially recall a long hike. I saw wild canaries, the first I had seen in five years, Baltimore orioles, and white and milky blue butterflies. The fragile strength of these airy creatures did wonders for my spirits.

Some Nice Things You Can Do for Yourself

To cope with stress, you have to learn to do something that some superstars find difficult: take time out for yourself. Spoil yourself a little, even. Taking that slow stroll down a country road is just one way.

Do you like to daydream? Fine, but don't build yourself a world of fantasy. You need to fashion dreams that can be translated into a better reality for yourself, your family, your friends, your associates, and the society you live in. Keep a sense of balance. Workaholics may pile up fortunes. In fact, many of them are the richest residents of Forest Lawn.

Keep on Learning

Research on longevity has demonstrated that getting more education is one of the best things we can do to prolong life. It is also one of the best things we can do to increase our effectiveness.

Maybe you cannot take a sabbatical or even attend a night class. You can still learn on your own. What's that? You say you don't have time? Just sit down and write down the things you do every week. You might come up with items like two trips to the hair stylist, two hours every day for lunch, three nights out for supper, golf on Wednesday, Saturday and Sunday, twelve hours of TV, and six hours working crossword puzzles.

Now read the list out loud to yourself. Doesn't it sound

silly? Okay, so edit your list. Edit the way a rewriter at the city desk does with a long-winded speech. Then add up the hours you have pared off your original list. That total should provide you with enough time to read one of Frank Bettger's books in a week, plus time left over to spend with your family.

Stay with your self-education program for the magic habit-forming period of six days. By that time you will have reason to be proud of yourself. What is even better, you will most likely start looking around for even more study time. You will start asking yourself questions like, "What am I doing watching the losers on 'Dallas' or 'Fantasy Island' "?

You should be the most exciting person you will meet in the next ten years. As you expand your horizons you won't have time to get worked up about the phony celebrities who fill the talk shows, sports pages, and gossip columns. Learning will make you grow, teach you to handle more challenges, increase your capacity for handling new problems, and give you a better edge on stress.

Be Yourself

Many people cause unnecessary stress with their efforts to keep up with the Joneses. Forget about the Joneses. For all you know, they may have been trying to keep up with *you*. If they actually are ahead, it is because they are minding their own business. That usually gives anyone an edge.

We are all unique. Like snowflakes, there are no two of us alike. Even so-called identical twins are different. This is especially important in the workplace. Many managers attempt to force their people into preconceived roles. I have gone through the agony of being pushed into the sausage grinder of strong-willed but weak-minded managers. It did not work. I allowed myself to be ground into near-anonymity until I realized that I really did not want to become human hamburger served up to suit someone else's taste.

When I became accustomed to working at what I wanted, in the way I wanted, most of my bouts with stress became simple sparring matches.

Many employees eventually fall victim to what I call overhead stress. I use the term for two reasons. Too many managers have pushed me into situations that were over my head; and too many people could go over my head to foul up further what I already could not handle.

One way to eliminate overhead stress is to go to work for yourself. As a bird in the corporate nest you are fed and protected by the parent eagles—or too often crows or pigeons. If you are afraid to fly on your own, you will be thrown out of the nest anyway. Of course going it on your own has its pitfalls, but they can be evaded if you read, think, and inquire enough.

If you are one of the fortunates who work under intelligent management you may be able to do a super job. The IBMs, GMs, and other giants need superstars and pay them well. If you can do what you set out to do while climbing the corporate ladder, you may prefer to remain an organization person.

I strongly suspect, however, that certain women and men are meant to capitalize on their uniqueness and control their own destinies.

As a loner you greatly reduce your causes for stress. Alone or with a company you have your family. (In case you think you should break out of the marital corral as well as the corporate pen, forget it. You may be ready for freedom from overhead stress, but liberation from family is not really yours to decide.)

Your clients will remain potential sources of stress. There is no reason why you should keep on cutting your own throat. Again, you can eliminate much self-stress by eliminating things you should not do and by adding those you should do. Impossible clients can either be cut off your list or handled by remote control. You can do this easier when you are on your own. There is no sales manager to tell you to "spend more time on the Snake Pit account." Also the

80/20 principle will probably work in your favor: the nicest people will give you 80 percent of your business, and your nastiest clients will barely give you 20 percent, while generating 80 percent of your expense and stress.

Give Worry a Vacation

Sometimes it is necessary to worry. A wise counselor on teenage sexual matters told his audience: "When someone says don't worry, honey—*worry!*"

In most cases, however, worry is just mismanaging tomorrow, today. Today has enough challenges and opportunities to enable us to stockpile problems.

Too many people are so certain they have some dangerous physical malady that they worry themselves sicker than they really are. I once was dead certain that I was afflicted with a serious heart ailment. I drove 35 miles to see a doctor friend who tapped, listened, and took x-rays. All that came to light was that my rib cage was a bit chewed up as a result of some of my less graceful skiing exploits.

Worries are often as silly as mine, but even when there is genuine cause for alarm you can still win the battle. Diving into a problem that won't go away is usually the best thing to do, but before you dive make sure there is water in the pool. In other words, be sure of your remedy. Get competent professional help if necessary.

I think my favorite worry story is one told by my friend, the late Bill North, who was both a charter-boat captain and a minister of the gospel. Sometimes his sermons were as salty as his experiences in the Florida Keys.

Many times he advised his flock not to worry, but I think he counseled them best with one of his stories. "Don't worry. You are either well, or you're sick. If you are sick, still don't worry. You're either going to get well, or you're going to die. If you die, don't worry. You will either go to heaven or to hell. So you go to hell. Still don't worry. You'll be so busy shaking hands with all your friends you won't have time to worry."

Focus on Your Goals

Worthwhile goals will give you the sense of direction that helps reduce stress. A lot of stress disappears when we get on track and know that we are headed the right way.

The late Jimmy Durante once did a beautiful lampoon on our aimlessness, our carelessness about establishing clear-cut goals. The skit involved Durante and a partner lost at sea in a small craft.

Durante asked his partner, "Whad'ya see?"

"Only the horizon."

"Make for dat, den."

Superstar sellers often move like homing pigeons or quarterhorses. Superstars know their goals and often speed up when drudges are looking for a quiet spot to cool off.

Ben Zolin, before he was gathered up by the prophets, was the kind of super seller who could take your breath away. A mutual friend once went with Ben on a tackle-selling jaunt among the fishing resorts of northern Minnesota. A relaxing change, visiting some of the 10,000 lakes, Ben's guest thought.

My friend had a very rude awakening at 5 A.M. There was just time for a quick clean-up, no time for breakfast. By 5:30 Ben was pounding at the door of the first resort, waking the owner and wife. Was he thrown out on his ear? Not on your life. Ben just walked in and complained about no breakfast on the table. He got breakfast, a nice order, and directions to the next resort. As I recall, the proprietors of the next lodge had breakfast ready. Ben could speed things up by just accepting another cup of coffee and writing up his second order for the day. A real superstar, who knew where he was going and wanted to get there fast.

Take Time for Preparation

Being prepared is another way of dodging stress. Superstars can wing it if need be, but usually they take time to get ready. They prepare for the future even if they do not know what is ahead.

Observe Your Sabbath

Even superstars can overdo it. Fifty percent of the people I know work on the Sabbath even though the best of laws says "No." You can get away with it once in a while, and sometimes it's necessary. But to make the Sabbath a regular part of your work schedule is a mistake to be avoided at all costs.

Some enterprises of their nature require Sunday work. If Salesperson Sal wants to ski on the weekend, Resorter Ruby has to be on deck to sell the tickets. Luckily for them, farmers and resorters normally get a chance to catch up during the off-season. Those who have no off-season should think the square root of twice before they preempt the Lord's day for making extra—and usually unneeded—bucks.

Keep Your Machinery Tuned Up

Physical fitness is one of your best anti-stress remedies. A sound mind is a treasure, but in a sound body it is a protected treasure. Also, your mind then becomes a usable treasure. If your body isn't functioning well, your mind isn't going to do you much good. We cannot take our brains to places where we can use them because our transportation system is broken down.

At almost any age most people can increase their mental output by getting into better condition. You may already be jogging, walking, swimming, or doing sitting-up exercises, but are you careful about what you put into your brain-buggy? Remember, your body is, in a sense, the mode of transportation for your brain. You wouldn't fill your car's gas tank with molasses. So why stuff your own fuel tank with too many sweets, too much salt, too much junk food, and junkier liquids?

It is much more expensive to bring your brain-buggy in for repairs than it is to repair your Mercedes. Spare parts for your body are also much harder to come by.

To take one more swing at the vehicle analogy, let us consider the problem of too much weight. A spendthrift can drive a heavy gas hog of a car if he wants to, but he will be outmaneuvered by a sprightly sports car. You people with too much weight know who you are. I won't tell on you, but your stomachs will. So will your decreased performance.

If you are overweight and underconditioned, you will be happily surprised at the unexpected dividends you get when you diet and exercise. On my current thinning and conditioning program I still have four pounds to go—I'm at 174 after starting at 200. The desired effects are already showing: my clothes fit better and my endurance is better. But there are some surprises:

1. My ankles (both were horribly clobbered in a plane crash) hardly ever scream for mercy. Four months ago I was using a cane. Now I'm thinking of fastening it to my fridge as a reminder of the bad old days.

2. I need less sleep. Now I am waking up about 5 A.M., sometimes a bit before.

3. I am going to take a friend of mine for a few dollars when our bet ends in another six weeks. The payoff, $1 per pound, will be based on the difference in our respective weight losses on weigh-in day. My friend doesn't think I am going to win. "Do not enumerate your juvenile poultry," he says "until the process of incubation is complete."

By the way, keeping your body in good condition is something that should never stop, not at any age. A few years ago, I accompanied Clyde Fickes of Missoula, Montana, on a very grueling 200-mile pack trip into Montana's

Bob Marshall Wilderness. Two of the pack animals did not even make it to our base camp. At the end of the first day, after 24 miles on the trail, Clyde helped set up camp. He looked fit enough to go for an evening hike.

Clyde made this trip when he was 90. One year later, age 91, he got married. Best wishes, Clyde.

Concentrate on Your Strengths

Let me tell you the secret many have found for a happy, stress-free life: do what you really like to do, and what you're good at, even it if means getting some more education.

I recall a period in my life when I rejected a chance to get some specialized education. I had already earned a college degree so I thought I didn't need it. What a mistake. The education would have cost me nothing. The lack of it cost me many gallons of blood, sweat, and tears. If I could have an opportunity to do it over, I would not only snatch at the chance to learn my job, I would insist on it. In fact, I would pay for it myself. I would go in debt for it.

Teachers sometimes make half-hearted efforts to convince their students that education is a lifelong process. Yet very few teachers—or parents, or managers—are geared to the search for talent. The girl who doodles pictures of her classmates should be urged to be more attentive, but she should also be encouraged to use her free time to develop her artistic talent.

Though many of us were short-changed by ineffective guidance and our own poor choices, we can still get back on track. Picking up a fumbled opportunity should also remove a cause for stress. Instead of giving yourself psychic kicks in the derriere for a missed opportunity, you will enjoy the thrill of correcting a mistake.

If you are a fast learner, you belong in the fast lane. You do not need to confine your learning to the art of selling and to product knowledge. You should keep up on what interests you. A hobby could become your way of making a living.

Your self-searching could lead you to suspect that you are pursuing the wrong career or pursuing it in the wrong way. Some literally hate their jobs or their situations.

Let us suppose you are 50 years old and selling cars. You are not national salesman of the year in the auto industry, but you have a nice home, eat well, and have been getting the kids through college. You could stay at your job until you retire. You might even be able to buy the business later on. Still, you're not happy. The task generates more stress every day.

You enjoy selling, but you are more interested in the financial world than you are in the automotive business. You think you could sell stocks and bonds, insurance, or tax shelters. You particularly admire insurance salespersons. You like the idea of helping others provide for their own security.

But when you look at what you have and at what you risk losing, you are too scared to think of changing. "If I fail," you tell yourself, "I will lose everything. I'll be out on the street."

Actually, the transition doesn't have to be all that hard. It may seem like diving off the high board into icy Lake Superior, but the change could be gradual. Talk it over with your sales manager. He could even be hoping you would make a change.

Even if you have to quit cars "cold turkey" to get into insurance, it would still be worth a try. The same could be true for an insurance seller whose first love is sports cars.

If you still are terrorized by a drastic career or lifestyle change, I suggest you read the best book I know on the subject. It helped me, and it can help you. You could easily read it in two hours: *How to Be Your Own Best Friend*, by Mildred Newman and Bernard Berkowitz. This short little book is one of the best tips in this whole chapter—the whole book, maybe. If you are inspired to read it, you will have more than recovered the price of this volume.

Once you zero in on what you like best you will, in a short time, also be doing your best. Baseball star Jim Kaat was transformed from a good pitcher into a star hurler by a good bit of advice from his coach. Kaat spent a lot of time trying to improve his two worst pitches, but his coach said, "Spend eighty to ninety percent of your time pitching your fast ball, because that's where you're good."

Concentrate on what you are good at, and you will have less stress. It is less tiring to be successful, and we need all the victories we can get to make up for the discouragement of defeat.

Money—the Biggest Stress of All

Managing money skillfully—avoiding debt and making intelligent spending decisions—has been known to bring on more stress than probably any other single element of modern life.

Debts sometimes must be incurred. Even wealthy farmers have to borrow up to and sometimes more than $1 million. I guess they have to be optimists; otherwise they would not be gambling on the weather and prices.

Sellers also have to be optimists, but they can let their optimism carry them away sometimes. If you buy too many things you really do not need, you could wind up with too heavy a debt load. This is bound to worry you. (If it does *not* worry you to be over your head in debt, you had better start worrying about your attitude—or maybe your ethics.)

The kind of debt that would worry me, and should worry you, is an amount that does not diminish as it should. It may even grow as you fight to reduce it.

It would be simple to say, "Well, get out and close more sales," but even finding the time to make more calls is not necessarily the answer. If you're fretting over your overdue bills and loans, you are not likely to have the verve you need to sell.

If you cannot figure out how to reduce the debt, talk to a good banker or counselor. Sometimes an objective person can show you that your "necessities" are actually waste.

I once counseled a young couple faced with an ultimatum from their credit bureau demanding immediate payment. Very early in the interview I learned that the wife spent a minimum of $60 a month to phone her mother—an amount that would have more than serviced the couple's debt. For her, trimming the phone bill was as frightening as falling out of a tree. The poor girl had never really left her nest. Her phone was the next best thing to being home with her mother.

In this case, getting out of debt was as easy—or as difficult—as it is to grow up. For anyone hopelessly in debt, even more drastic and difficult steps could be necessary. Are you superstar enough to quit drinking, stop trying to be a clothes horse, say goodbye to the poker club, drive a compact car, or eat out only once a month? Overindulgence in anything is one of the best debt builders known. By cutting down on your wining, dining, partying, and high living in general you will pad your pocketbook and help unpad your hips.

Try this on to see if it fits. The only reason you have for staying at a $50-a-night hotel is to have a nice bar and supper club handy. You tell yourself you need the exercise in the pool, but after you sign for a $7 bar bill you are never in the mood to use the available swimming facilities. You feel you owe yourself a good supper to compensate for the loneliness of the crowded city. After all, you only spent $19 for lunch in the hotel; your client had only one martini. Supper and breakfast plus two magazines adds $27 to your bill. The clerk at the check-out desk presents you with a bill for $103. It goes on your travel card, so it seems painless.

It may seem to make a difference if you can put everything on an expense account. I do not look on it that way. There is a rule, much neglected, but still on the books: "Do unto others as you would have them do unto you." Unless your employer specifically designates sumptuous overnight accommodations you should treat them just as you would if you were paying your own way.

Most superstar sellers, of course, prefer to work on commissions and pay their own expenses. If you are one of this type, or are entirely on your own, you are now ready to get out of debt. If your expense pattern is at all like the one just outlined, you can easily cut your hotel bill in half. First off, stay in a $25 room. The cheaper hotel does not have a pool, but it also does not have a bar. You save $7 on calorie-rich booze. A walk down a well-lighted street will relax you. (If you are afraid of muggers, do some calisthenics in your room.) Your shower will feel better than the swim you never took at the expensive hotels. To save the $2 cost of magazines, you read the book you never found time for. For lunch you cut $7 on liquor by taking your client to a restaurant that has no bar. Maybe you cannot shave much off breakfast, but by going back to the place where you had lunch you cut $13 off your supper bill.

You add up your savings: hotel, $25 saved; no bar-flying, $7; lunch, $12; supper and magazines, $15. Your total saving is $59.

Two days on the road on this basis would give you $118 for debt reduction every week, $511 every month, and $6,136 per year. If you cannot cut your debt with $6,000 extra a year, maybe you should have one of your kids handle your finances. With $6,000, you could pay 16 percent interest for one year on a debt load of $37,500.

Maybe your weekly travel savings will not do it for your debt, but you have only scratched the surface when you replan your travel needs. A family conference might help. Why not announce the problem one night at supper, and ask everyone to bring money-saving ideas to a meeting to be held in two days? You might start things off by giving everyone an idea of how to go about it. Explain what you have already done with your expense account.

Another point that cannot be emphasized enough is that by reducing expenditures for self-indulgence, you increase both your net worth and also your value as a person. The economics I suggested on your road expenses will not deprive you of sleep or sustenance. You may even be able to sleep better in a more reasonable hotel.

Make Today a Success

Speaking of debts reminds me of what we owe besides money. Bankers and creditors have legal means of getting what is coming to them. Our creator, our parents, our families, our communities, our country, our companies, our customers, and many others have all contributed something of what we are, and they need to be repaid. A lot of people like to think they are self-made men or women. There are just as many self-made computers as there are self-made persons.

I try to be as spiritual a person as I can. I go to church because I want to pay my creator for my health, my mind, my family, and blessings too many to list. Some of the most successful people I have dealt with in the past half-century were faithful to their respective religious faiths. They kept the Ten Commandments. They loved their spouses and their children.

How many of us ever think of dropping in on an old teacher? Even teachers we disliked taught us something, so we owe them too. The years may have removed us too far from our former mentors for a personal "thank you." You may have no way of contacting them, but you can still make a payment by passing on some of what they taught you.

Showing how it is done is often more effective than the best lecture or sermon. You can start with your own kids. You can demonstrate manners, courtesy, patience, love, and self-control. You can also impart attitudes. Are your children worth enough to you to demonstrate abstinence from smoking? Are they worthy of a lifelong demonstration of sobriety?

Another payment you must not forget is to a future

person: you. In a given number of years you will want to retire. Health problems could move the date ahead for you. Now is the time to gild those so-called golden years. Social Security will help, but you will not travel very far on it. Surely you do not want to end up with all the leisure you ever wanted but nothing in your fun fund.

To a solo seller, the future is more of a concern than to one working for a company with a good pension plan. Worrying about the future possibility of disastrous medical bills is all too common. I know of no insurer, including the government, that offers complete disaster insurance for the possible long-term disability of you or your spouse. Probably you cannot adequately cover all contingencies, but right now you can do something at least. You accumulate a nest egg the same way you make up for eating your chickens before they hatch.

Maybe you cannot do much, but do what you can. Just taking action will reduce stress. Doing your best is a good antidote for anxiety. Doing one's best always seems to replace negative thoughts with a deserved feeling of satisfaction.

Whatever you do, I would suggest you read *The Richest Man in Babylon,* by George S. Clason, who believes that ten percent of everything you earn is yours to keep. It is not a long book, but it can make you hopeful of building a more secure future.

People who pay their monentary and social debts are gifted with a lighthearted approach to life that crowds out stress. They are too busy helping others to get upset about their own problems. In fact, givers and doers have fewer problems to cause stress.

Your struggles to rectify mistakes, break your own sales record, lose some pounds, lift an extra weight, learn a new closing, and add to your stock portfolio will not be easy. Any dummy can handle easy things.

When you succeed, celebrate. When you make the final payment on your car, take your spouse and kids to the beach. When your scale gives you the good news that you made your weight goal for the week, treat yourself to a massage. When I reach my goal of repeating a given exercise, say 20 times, I give myself a short round of applause. Silly? Not as silly as going unrewarded for an honest effort.

Do whatever is necessary to make today a success. Better yet, do what is necessary to make every moment as productive as you can. When you laugh, let it be hearty. When you eat, take time to ask God's blessing. When you kiss your spouse, pretend it is the first time.

Live life fully every minute. That way you lay the foundation for a good hour, a fine day, a wonderful week, a terrific month, a fabulous year, and an outstanding life.

CHAPTER 10

All That Dead Fish Get Is the Frying Pan

Superstar sellers are often mavericks: hard to handle, even temperamental. They do not always go through channels or follow protocol, and details just get in their way. Yet they sell four to five times as much as someone who meekly goes by the book. Because they don't spend a lot of time in conventional country-club circles, some observers call them "odd ducks." I think of them as being like wild ducks fresh from the Canadian subarctic. Watching these creatures flitting freely from swamp to flooded grain field, you might think them strange, but they know where they are going.

The sooner you get over the "follow-the-crowd" mentality, the sooner you will walk in the rarefied atmosphere of the superstar. I do not mean you should deliberately set out to be singular—"kooky," if you will. There are already far too many who flaunt their failure to handle reality. What I mean is that if you do just a few things correctly you will be a delightful and successful person. You will stand out from the crowd like the Washington Monument.

If you want to test this statement, stop and think. How many people do you know whom you have never heard tell a lie? How many who never talk unfavorably about someone who is not present? How many who do not overload themselves with too much food, drink, night life, and general self-indulgence? How many who will leave the TV set to study or write? How many who will go out of their way to help someone?

I guess what I want to say is that you must dare to be yourself, the kind of self your conscience and your upbringing tell you to be. To be part of the crowd is easy. To stand out from the mass of easygoing humanity, you must do what the crowd cannot do: think and act for yourself.

When you work on your own resources, building on what you already have with what you can and should do, you become a unique person. We cannot escape some of the shaping of our environment. In fact, it is not worth the trouble to try. It is worth the trouble, though, to build up the real you. The finished product will be a person who radiates authenticity. You will, in a sense, be a work of art: a genuine human being.

The Superstar and the Dead Fish

Superstars genuinely like people, and they show it in their enthusiasm and their attitude of aliveness. Unfortunately, too many sellers behave suspiciously like dead fish. You know what happens to dead fish, don't you? They end up in the pan—unless they have been dead too long.

Nobody likes to pet a wet fish. Neither does a customer

like to stroke something wet—whether fish, blanket, or personality. Did I ever tell you what Skinhead calls listless, barely alive nonentities? Well, on second thought, some other time maybe.

Judging from the number of surly, lackluster salespersons in the average store, I would say the dead-fish market has been oversold. We have all experienced handshakes that were as pleasant as grabbing a moray eel. People are tired of clerks who chew a sandwich at you or blow smoke in your face.

Superstars like to spend time with customers, and customers can sense it. You can also sense the other kind, especially when you are the only person in a store. You look for an item you know you want, but cannot quite describe it. A dead-fish clerk comes up and listlessly whines, "Can I help you?" You tell him as best you can. He makes a half-hearted survey of the shelves, but he can't find it because he knows little more about the stock than you do.

I once encountered a sales clerk in an office supply store who actually left me alone to search for the desired item. Meanwhile he walked to the front of the store. To work on the window display? Not by the hair on the pirate's wooden leg. The only thing he displayed was total indifference to his customer, his job, and probably his future. I say "probably" because he just stood there staring out at the street where his future was likely to be when the store owner finally caught on.

I am leaving it up to you to figure out why there were no customers in the paper-clip emporium when I walked in. Better yet, let one of the kids figure it out. The store is no longer in my old town. I think the owners went into the greenhouse nursery business—to give the employees more windows to stare out of.

The worst example of nonselling I ever encountered was in a pancake house in Key West, Florida. Skinhead and I were going out on an emergency fishing trip at 8 A.M., and we wanted to get in and out of the breakfast nook as quickly as possible. As we sat down in a booth to prepare for our public service mission, we saw a few other early birds but no one to wait on customers. We waited for a waiter—and waited and waited. Then our fuses started their countdown. Before any explosion could occur, a cook sang out, "Orders are ready." Three waitresses popped out of a booth and headed for the kitchen. Skinhead and I headed for the door. Neither of us could stand sellers who hide from customers instead of looking for business.

Always Lay a Red Carpet for Your Customer

All sellers need to be aware of what I sometimes call the red carpet rule. In essence, it means making yourself easily available and making the path to you as pleasant and as easy as possible. Availability is a concept that can generate the kind of thinking you need to draw business to you. Laying a red carpet is symbolic of a warm, royal welcome.

One fishing camp operator in Canada actually carpeted his dock area in a plush red. When guests left their seaplane they followed the baggage handlers up a well-brushed red carpet to the camp area. The plush treatment continued for the duration of their stay.

I suppose it is physically as easy to walk on a gray or even a soiled carpet, but psychologically I would find it easier on the royal red. Its crimson richness tells me that I am royally welcomed. That means a lot to someone who is already ill at ease because of new surroundings. Some Firestone stores have areas for customers waiting for their cars. A nearby coffee urn with an ample supply of throw-away cups accents the voice of welcome.

Anything that will make a new customer feel welcome makes you more accessible. Your store should be designed so that you or your department heads quickly come to the rescue when something gets fouled up or when all the clerks are busy—or loafing.

Managers can use waiting areas as an opportunity to cultivate known big spenders and to develop new ones.

Anything you can do to put yourself nearer your buyers or potential customers will make credit, new opportunities, travel, philanthropy, and all the good things of life more accessible to you.

Any customer, friend, or advisor can give you many suggestions for improving your accessibility. I recently went to a large department store to buy picture-hanging hardware. It was not in the logical place with the picture frames so I asked a swiftly moving clerk. All she did was say, "Hardware" and point to the area. In about five minutes I located the proper shelf, but it was not completely stocked. In another minute I would have left the store and headed for a small hardware store down the road a few blocks.

Based on my experience in the huge find-it-yourself stores, I would suggest a few ways to make it easier for shoppers to meet the desired merchandise.

Put up cross-reference signs on racks of goods that could be associated with other things in the store: at a rack of frames, set up a notice advising that hanging equipment will be found in the hardware department. Your manner of associating things is probably different from mine, but I would have a reference sign near the fishing tackle giving the location of mosquito lotion, Band-Aids, and liquid refreshments.

In one grocery supermarket the carts have long poles attached. I suppose they serve the same purpose as elevated flags on motor cars: so their owners can find them in parking lots. The high shelves usually seem to have enough altitude to hide the Boston Celtics. The tip of an unmoving pole might well help a frantic shopper find her lost cart.

I am not suggesting the attachment of similar poles to the persons of clerks and other store hands. Yet what would be wrong with asking workers to carry an elongated staff that could easily be seen above the high cliffs of merchandise? Sure this is a screwball idea, but so was the wild scheme of letting buyers wander at will among the shelves.

Call buttons might be attached to shelves so that a

bewildered shopper could send out an S.O.S. Corresponding beepers could be attached to the responsible clerk. A second button could also be attached to the shelf, bearing the instruction, "If no answer push this button." An on-the-ball clerk is not going to indulge in too many long coffee breaks knowing that some pushy customer could go over her or his head.

Make sure the warmth of your attitude matches your approach carpet. I remember a cartoon depicting a welcome rug guarded by a snarling cur. You can make yourself as accessible as a housefly and just as obnoxious if you lack basic courtesy.

This is one of the most hard-to-find virtues. It is as scarce as the superstar seller. In fact, when you find a superstar salesperson, you have found a lady or a gentleman.

The Good Side of Nonselling

Of course there are times when *not* selling something is the best thing you can do. A genuine superstar knows how to tell the difference. My broker, Doug Schwartz of Grand Forks, North Dakota, is a prime example.

Just recently, Doug cemented his attraction for me by *not* trying to sell me anything. I had some extra funds that I thought I would use to build up my portfolio, so I asked Doug what hot item he had to recommend. "Nothing special," he said, and let it go at that. Since I know about as much about stocks as I do about Sanskrit, I was at his mercy. I had the cash in my hot little hand, so if he had recommended Bifurcated Oyster Beds I would have placed an order.

By that one "no-sale," Doug Schwartz closed at least a few future sales with me. I hope it can be a considerable number.

Next time you encounter any dead fish (even in the bathroom mirror), tell it to go jump in the nearest lake. You have only one mortal life. No one gets to come back. Take hold of this one. Give life a friendly squeeze. Life is like anything else. It likes to be loved. Now is the time to start the most fascinating, rewarding, and profitable courtship of your career.

CHAPTER 11

Nobody Buys a Castle in the Sky

Whenever someone opens up a peanut stand and quickly starts talking about setting up national franchises, I get very nervous. They don't realize that before making it big they have to make it good.

Nobody buys a castle in the sky. You have to build something substantial in the real world to sell to down-to-earth people. Let the do-nothing dreamers build the moonbeam mansions.

The transition from the wispy stuff of dreams to the substance of reality is often an agonizing process, and a lot of hearts and heads are broken in the attempt.

Learning from the Experiences of Others

For those who have not gone through the agony of launching a new business, I am going to turn you over to a valiant young woman who launched her own specialty shop. Sandy Ellen Opp of Eureka, South Dakota tells her own story.

> I've been the owner, manager, and buyer of The Gentry in Eureka, South Dakota, for seven years. It is a specialty shop retailing juniors' and womens' fashions.
>
> My home economics degree in textiles and clothing and actual on-the-job experience in a large retailing firm in Dallas gave me an excellent background in this business. However, it did not prepare me for the struggles of being self-employed in a small business. I knew the complexities of big business and had yet to learn to operate my own small shop in a much different manner. It's been a challenging transition. Things which I knew worked in high volume traffic just did not apply in my business. Add a slow economy and high interest rates. Each year I found myself deeper in debt and working harder but getting nowhere.
>
> I worked extremely hard with promotions and fashion shows knowing I could compete on a high level anywhere. Yet I was not getting the immediate business spurt which I needed. The slack was somewhat due to my dependency on the farm economy in our area.
>
> It just seemed impossible to weigh the input versus the output of advertising. It seemed so left-to-chance. I just was not able to control the results without spoiling my customers by giving things away and getting myself deeper in trouble.
>
> Meanwhile, the quality of clothing, display, and all facets of business were outwardly improving a great deal. However, because of the tough economy, the customer was demanding more and more sales and making me feel guilty about my prices. I found myself dropping prices constantly just to free money to pay bills and stay in business.

Mr. Sheehan taught me never to apologize or feel guilty for my prices and merchandise. He has helped me to gain control of the selling situation. I had become quite experienced as a buyer, but lacked some of the essential traits of the true salesperson.

Knowing the future was not in my hands, but God's, I asked myself many times over why I was in business. I truly enjoyed the challenge of retailing, but I was tired of not getting anywhere. However, I felt that my business had great potential, but just needed something extra to make it really successful and lower my debt. I prayed for an answer.

Mr. Sheehan's course was the answer. His whole concept of business and life could not have fit more perfectly with mine. His expertise and experience were all he needed to share.

Now I have applied his facts and figures concerning direct mail. I now have more control of my business than ever before. Business is more stable. By making my mailings a monthly event I have increased my business from 30 to 50 percent a month in the heart of my major seasons.

This, however, is still somewhat dependent on the weather and economy. For example, when I ran my big early spring sale this season there was a blizzard and bad road conditions for several days and things just never got off the ground. Last year, however, my business increase in the same month was phenomenal. At this point business was crucial and direct mail made the difference.

Suddenly, the goals which I set were becoming realities—not years away but now. I began really to know who my customers were. I quit complaining about the poor economy and customers who didn't shop here. My mailing list was growing and growing.

I had been compiling a mailing list for some time and yet did not realize its worth until attending Mr. Sheehan's courses. In order to increase my clientele I worked with other people in the area to update my lists and obtain leads on good, new potential customers.

Mr. Sheehan teaches the lost art of salesmanship,

which is something I always wanted to delve into. For years I knew that I probably shopped the market many times over compared to my competition. Now I'm much more secure in my business. I'm very excited about the future and know that by dedication and hard work coupled with this new knowledge I will be successful, God willing.

I hope always to be remembered as a professional who offered our area well-priced, quality fashions, not just to customers but to people who became friends and felt the same loyalty as I felt for them.

A Short Course in Realty

Now, there is what I call dealing with reality. Ms. Opp demonstrated the basic realities of selling in a straightforward, convincing manner.

1. *She discovered she needed know-how. She got it as quickly as she possibly could.*
2. *She learned she could not be diffident about asking for her prices. She decided what she had to get, set her prices, and got them.*
3. *She understood the need for promotion. She cranked out more and more mail. People read and liked what they learned.*
4. *She used imagination and creative thinking. You read her letter. You saw a superstar's mind in action.*
5. *She knew it would take hard work to put it all together. She proved herself a top-shelf realist.*

There is another bit of reality that I would like to present as a sidebar to Ms. Opp's heart-warming story: women can more than hold their own in the world of retailing.

First, Get Started

When Ms. Opp struck out on her own, she had a lot of experience, more than many others who set up in business. I would say she was justified in taking the plunge.

People who make the attempt to prepare for every contingency become procrastinators. There has to be a happy medium. We don't want to start something without weighing our chances and learning everything we can. But getting started is probably even more important. You are going to make some bad guesses about products, about promotional techniques, about start-up money, about a lot of things. Even people who are solidly established in business do not know all the answers, but they know enough of them to help noncompeting entrants into their own or similar fields. One of the advantages of going into a franchised venture is the know-how that quickly becomes available to you.

Add to Your Know-How

When Ms. Opp found herself plagued with a poor cash flow, she was smart enough and audacious enough to gamble the price of a training course.

Realistically, you are going to make mistakes. Equally realistically, you will get nowhere crying about them. The same intelligence and audacity that got you into what seems like a mess is available to get you out of it.

Reality is often cold and tough. It may even seem to be an enemy, but it is really neutral. If you can master your portion of reality it will work for you.

Learn When to Say NO

I once went into a small publishing venture with a pair of fast-talking promoters. They were nice, friendly, and even competent in some phases of publishing: graphics, layout, and printing. They were also adept at fast talking, lying, and high living.

My grasp of reality was weaker than theirs. Finally, they admitted that they could not pay back my $11,000. They filed bankruptcy. All I got out of it was the notice.

Well, not only the notice. I learned a lot about reality. As the years passed, I discovered that a little two-letter word is indispensable in dealing with some realities: "no." It can save a lot of heartache and a lot of sad statements.

Don't Be Afraid to Ask Your Price

Getting her prices was another reality that Ms. Opp quickly grasped. She realized that selling and social work are too different things. In selling, you make the money; in social work, your client makes the money.

I recall one super seller who bought two war-surplus planes and a boxcar-load of spare parts for $30,000. One of the planes was in top working order. Jake kept it for himself, and put the other plane up for sale at $32,000.

When a buyer laid a check for $30,000 on Jake's desk, Jake just handed it back. "Sorry, the price is $32,000. I'm not in the charity business." After a trip to Texas to look at another similar plane, the buyer came back with a new check. It was made out for the correct amount.

Promotion Is an Essential Investment

The reality of promotion cannot be stressed enough. Even the kid who sets up a lemonade stand knows enough to put up a sign.

Promotion, like it or not, is a ladder that has no top. As long as you are in business, you must keep on promoting. You must be continually on the alert for new ways to spread your gospel.

Put out a suggestion box, and try to show some recognition to anyone who tries to help. If you are a solo operator or, as in my case, a family effort, set up a box at home. If no one comes up with an idea tell the kids to take the box to school. At least you will get young ideas.

Our rapidly changing world calls for new approaches. You should consider yourself lucky if you do not have to revamp your entire product or service line. Promotion is always going to be part of your selling life—like death and taxes, but much more profitable.

Mind you, I am talking about just staying business. To grow is even more difficult. The bigger you get, the more effort you must make to keep from sliding back. To gain on the pursuing wolves of obsolescence, change, recession, competition, and changing habits and tastes, you must keep your promotional task vigorous.

As an unknown author put it: "If the going is getting easier, you are not climbing."

You'll Never Avoid Hard Work

The reality of hard work is, there's no way around it. But hard work builds stamina and strength.

Learning to type is hard work. So is digging for new business. So is closing. It becomes easier once you sweat through a new sales talk, a new closing approach.

Building a good business is like building a good body. You eliminate the unneeded fat of costly inventory that does not move. Presto! You find it easier to sell the good things in your line.

As you toughen up your selling muscles, it becomes easier to coordinate them and much more fun. Your laughter becomes heartier on your way to the bank.

★★★★★★★★★ **CHAPTER 12** ★★★★★★★★★

Almost Any Dummy Can Do It Alone

There are really only two ways you can make big money. One is by selling big-ticket items: ships, skyscrapers, companies, or bridges—like Brooklyn's, maybe. The second way is by arithmetic: multiplying your own effectiveness by adding other people who can sell as well as you can, even better maybe. You are more likely to make real money by this self-multiplication route. The more good people you can delegate work to, the more time to work you'll have. And as soon as you are spending more time working, you will find that you are making more profits.

Delegating Is Smarter than Doing It Yourself

One of the first advocates of delegating work was not a professor from the Harvard Business School. Nor was it Adam Smith. It wasn't even one of the leaders of the Industrial Revolution.

You may pause here to guess. Not too long, because you are not going to get it anyway.

It was Moses. His father-in-law, Jethro, had come to Mount Sinai to visit. On the second day of his visit, Jethro observed that Moses stayed at his task of administering justice "from morning till evening."

Moses had a good reason for his long hours: "Because the people come to me to bring their enquiries to God. . . . I settle the differences between the one and the other and instruct them in God's statutes and His decisions."

This was not good enough for Jethro: "It is not right . . . to take this on yourself. You will tire yourself out, you and the people with you. The work is too heavy for you. You cannot do it alone. Take my advice and God will be with you. Teach them the statutes and decisions . . . but choose from the people at large some God-fearing men, trustworthy and incorruptible. . . . Let these be at the service of the people to administer justice at all times. They can refer all difficult questions to you, but all smaller questions they will decide for themselves."

Moses, being both a very wise person and a very good listener, took the advice, and thus established the judicial system of the Israelites.

There are few things more nerve-racking than working your head off and winding up at the end of the day with a bigger backlog of work than there was in the morning. You get to the point where there are no more working hours you can add to your day. So as your surrogate father-in-law, I am telling you to delegate as much as you can to as many good people as you can find. Then make sure that it gets done.

Give Your Job Away

Last year I worked for eleven millionaires. Without even trying, they taught me that delegation is the way to get things off our shoulders. A very wealthy Minneapolis man told me, "It is my job every day to give parts and bits of my job away. I try to give it away so that it frees me up to do the things I want."

Probably you're not exactly thrilled about giving away your job. It is doubly difficult to do when it is work that you like and think you can do much better than anyone else. You have to do it, though. You need to free yourself for creative planning. Your effort will pay out in:

1. *More planning time and a chance to determine where your company is headed.*
2. *More relaxation and job enjoyment.*
3. *More time for vacation free of worry about whether the job is getting done.*
4. *A better vantage point from which to monitor your entire operation: human relations, evaluating customers, quality control, and the effectiveness of your promotions.*
5. *More time to think, to put your imagination to work.*
6. *A trained replacement so you can move up.*

Basically you have two choices: delegate or stagnate. A good, intelligent effort to give your job away will pay off with superstar employees and super growth.

But First, Do You Really Need Help?

Before you turn over the work you have been doing yourself, you must be certain that you really *need* assistance. Make sure that it is not just an ego kick. A desire to command is not enough. There also has to be enough to do. There is a law that covers the negative side of delegation in a very concise way. It is known as Parkinson's Law: "Work expands to fill the time allotted for it." It is elaborated in C. Northcote Parkinson's wise and witty book, *Parkinson's Law*. The expansion of your staff can be the breaking or the making of you. So my advice is, take time to read his book. It should be in the library of anybody with a staff of one or more persons.

I have seen far too many examples of Parkinson's Law in action. One of the most recent involved a fraternal organization that was trying to get out of the doldrums. At the urging of another member, I dropped in at the club rooms. There were seven people in the lounge: the manager, the bartender, and five customers. It was well into the happy hour in a fairly thirsty town, but the crowd did not grow by as much as one more thirst during the thirty minutes I was there. When I left, the bartender had the same five customers, two at the bar and three playing cards with the manager.

Though I am a member of this lodge I have never gone back. I was afraid that the bartender might have hired someone to wash glasses—all six of them. I just could not have endured it. Now the lads will have to play elsewhere. The lodge has been reduced to an office. There no longer is a lounge or dining room.

The moral to this story could have been written by Parkinson himself: Your motives for adding to your work force must be sound. Don't hire someone just so you can play cards with the customers.

The Basic Rule of Three

If the idea of managing a staff is new to you, it might seem fairly overwhelming at first. I'm not going to try to tell you there's nothing to it, but you can break it down into manageable hunks.

You really don't have to coddle people who want to work—and you aren't going to have any other kind, right?

Your delegation must be the no-nonsense type. It is up to you to provide something of value for your people to sell. Then treat them fairly. You have to be able to assign tasks, and you must be able to tell when the work is properly done. You need to reward good work, and tactfully correct mistakes.

I like to think of delegation as the Rule of Three.

1. You must hire people who are used to hard work. Sometimes applicants have a seasoned look about them, but check their references anyway. Every minute you spend finding the right person will save countless hours later on. Then train them thoroughly in your particular job.

2. Do your best to hold your employees' interest and loyalty. Talk to your people. Get them excited enough about what you are doing so they want to stay. It is mighty discouraging to train workers to do a good job, and then have them walk off with the skill you gave them. It's even worse when they take your know-how to a competitor.

3. You must equip your staff for optimum performance. Make sure you actually transfer enough authority and responsibility to get the job done; too many managers give responsibility but hold back on authority. This means setting them up to do such a good job that they eventually become eligible for advancement. If your people do not grow, you do not grow.

Hiring the Best

I am not going to try to tell you that hiring help is simple. If it were, anyone could run General Motors. But it's not overly formidable either. What you have to do is the same as the successful companies do. They consider the sources of their information; they check applicants; they try them out on actual work.

There's an old saying that every personnel director should follow: "You can't make a silk purse out of a sow's ear." Another way of saying the same thing is so simple that you should almost be able to catch the meaning in the original Latin: *Nemo dat quod non habet.* ("No one gives what one does not have.")

Managers should exercise more care in hiring an employee than they do in buying their cars. Smart vehicle buyers get a mechanic to go over a used car or make a thorough study of available new cars. Some just want serviceable cars. Others want the most expensive one they can afford; they are interested in both quality and prestige.

Your choice of an employee has to be more important than the purchase of a machine. The human being you choose will be affected by you. So will his or her family. You also will be affected by your employee. To let a fellow human being get into an unsatisfactory situation with little chance of success is inhumane. It is also unprofitable.

Before I became fully aware of the precautions needed in engaging a new staff member I made a few bad choices. Two of them—highly recommended college graduates— stand out in memory.

Number one was recommended by a friend in my line of work. My friend had had to let this person go, but thought he could do a good job for me. As it happened, the new employee was a worse handicap for my business than for his former employer.

It turned out, however, that he had a real aptitude for accounting, which he was neither trained nor hired to do. I learned this when, in desperation, I turned over an auditing problem that I could not untangle. He solved it. At that stage in the development of my business, I did not need a full-time bookkeeper, so I had to let him go. As we parted, I suggested he pursue something in line with his newly discovered talent.

My second big hiring boner involved a young woman just out of college. This time I went through a personnel placement agency. The recommendations from the university, her major adviser, and the agency were glowing. I had to put on dark glasses to read her resume.

In a month she was through, and I was stuck with a substantial placement fee.

She could not, or would not, do the work she was hired to

do. What she did instead was have her husband call in sick for her as often as she felt like it. If I had had her for longer than a month, I would have been calling in sick too.

I discovered later that her college adviser had told his students to "do your own thing." I have some advice of my own for that professor: In the real world you do your employer's thing.

I am not an anti-intellectual by any means, but I find that it is often harder to get a college graduate on track than a high-school-trained person. Typically, typists will finish high school not knowing how to spell and quite satisfied with C-grade work. But I have generally been successful in convincing them that there are no such things as grades in business letters: they are either right or they are wrong. College graduates can usually spell better and speak more fluently, but they do not listen as well as high school trainees. Too often their stuffed egos get stuck between their ears.

Interviewing Recruits

When you check out a candidate, set a good scene: soft drinks and coffee (but no booze—you don't want anyone to think you're running a country club). You want the applicant to be relaxed. Maybe your office is too formidable. In that case change to neutral territory: the cafeteria, the coffee room, the conference room, or the little café down the street.

When you show interest in the applicant you will help remove any remaining tension. You are also going to get a lot more information when you show genuine interest.

The applicant did not really come to get your opinions. So listen, don't lecture. Save that for the Rotary meeting when you are asked to talk on "The Interviewing and Employing of Superstars."

Make sure you ask all the necessary questions. We are prohibited by law from asking about such things as race, police records, or religious preference. But maybe you need to know whether the applicant can drive a car or fly an airplane. Most salespersons need to drive to do their job. A few can make their assignments by using the airlines and taxis, but driving a car is almost as basic as speaking English in this country. Maybe a pilot's license is less common, but it sure helps sometimes. I knew a detail man who sold surgical supplies to widely scattered hospitals and clinics. The last time I saw him, he covered his widespread territory in fair weather and foul with his 200-mile-an-hour private plane.

As soon as you have all the information you can get, take it someplace where you can't be bothered; your private office, home, the library, or a church. And take your time. You're about to make a serious decision.

There are no buttons to push for an instantaneous estimation of people. Nor can you simply go by appearance. Good-looking people sometimes rely too much on their personal scenery. Plain folks often pass them in the learning process. A tall, attractive person could be the laziest and the hardest to teach.

Assume Nothing; Check Everything

It could be that your applicant is no longer with her or his former employer because of a failure to perform. Applicants may claim to have had special training courses. Check their know-how anyway; maybe they were daydreaming in class. A worthwhile applicant should not mind a probationary period before a contract is signed.

One of the best ways to find out about an applicant is to check with customers your applicant has served. Some managers use employees to help make an evaluation, but there is always the possibility that your old hand may be threatened by a newcomer. A customer has less reason for bias.

You may have to spend a little extra in selecting your

people. Medical circles call it preventive medicine. On a limited talent-search budget I would sometimes use psychologists. Unlike personnel agencies, they do not collect their commissions on the basis of your employees' wages. They evaluate applicants; you pay a fee for their service. A large food chain depends on psychologists when hiring management trainees. One of the chain's managers told me that a group of twenty likely candidates yielded only five people who were psychologically fit for the chain's kind of management.

Actually, over the years I have found that the best way to pick good employees is to get them to pick you. Candidates for a new job, if they are smart, will size up your store, your plant, your policies, your other employees, and *you*. If they do not do that, they are probably not smart enough to work for you.

You Get What You Pay For

When you're hiring new talent, you have to face the question of salary. A good, sound payment policy will attract the people you want. To put it another way, first class is often a better bargain than cut-rate. It is less expensive in the long run to buy the most expensive furniture you can find. The top-grade pieces will look better, last longer, and have a much better resale than the "El Cheapo" brand. I once took a trip to Lusaka, Zambia, on tourist class. Later I learned that first class would have cost only $400 more. For that I would have had 20 pounds more baggage allowance, the use of first-class lounges, the customary first-class frills, and many more options for rerouting my return trip.

It's just as true for people as it is for furniture or airline service—when you try to go cut-rate, that's what you get. If you want the best, you have to pay for it. In the end, it's the best bargain.

So You've Hired 'Em—Now What?

Once you decide you want someone, your work is just
starting. Now you have to begin the task of managing . . . of
training your new hand in how you want the job done, and
inspiring and encouraging the best possible performance.

I would suggest you set up a little sign on your desk, or
maybe on your bathroom mirror, someplace where you can
see it every day. Just print out three letter *i*'s. Not capitals,
the big *I* is too egotistical. It should look about like this: *i-i-
i.*

They stand for a trio of management musts: instruct,
inspire, and insist. You *instruct* with manuals, visual aids,
seminars, and coaching. You *inspire* with good example,
decent pay, and considerate treatment. You *insist* by firmly
following through on your instructions and by your consistency in demanding performance from everyone—even relatives, if they're in your employ.

Good Orientation Sets the Stage

If you're smart, the first thing you'll give a new employee is a thorough orientation to your company. At one
large plant, turnover was cut 60 percent by a half-day
program of introduction to the president, the comptroller,
all the departments, the secretaries, and the other employees.

Special attention should be given to the role for which
your new hand is slated. If the new person replaces someone just promoted, that person can help you develop a good
description of the job. The duties should be described,
demonstrated, and outlined in writing. There is no reason I
can think of why the new employee should not be given a
short quiz. It will help impress your new employee with
your efficiency and with your no-nonsense approach, and
you may discover a fast learner.

In your briefing give enough of a picture to fit the employee into the proper niche, more if time permits. Some general knowledge should also be given. The fill-in should include, besides details about the department, the number of employees, the volume of your promotional mail, your advertising program, your sales volume, and the companies you represent or serve.

The orientation process can be made easier if you provide a work manual. If you don't already have one, get started on it now. Write down the rules you expect to be observed. Ask you managers, your sales directors, your foremen to study these rules and make suggestions for additions or subtractions.

For instance, if trucks are to leave your plant or warehouse at 7 A.M., your drivers obviously cannot show up at 7:10 A.M. In fact they had better get there at 6:30 to make sure their trucks are properly loaded and serviced.

Vacation, sick leave, bonuses, raises, and fringe benefits should all be spelled out. Good work rules and company policies make it possible for your people to know where they stand. It makes it easier for you too. If someone breaks a rule or wants something not outlined in your company manual, you do not have to hem and haw. The answer is there in black and white.

The first 1,000 words you say to your new hand are more important than the next 10,000. Wherever possible, I like to use a few slides in a orientation session. Slides are visible notes; they remind you of items you might otherwise forget. Slides can also demonstrate seasonal products or activities in your branches that you can't show in person.

By this time your trainee should know you mean business, but it does not hurt to put into words your demand for good performance. Then continually check on things. It shows you care, and that you expect good work.

With new employees, daily communications will usually give you better rapport, and better results. Even after they've been with you for a while, you should continue to monitor new workers' performance. I became the number one producer, worldwide, for Dale Carnegie Associates, largely because one of its vice presidents wrote or phoned me from New York every month over a period of three years.

Tell Them What to Do, Then Tell Them Again

Training is probably the most important ingredient in delegation. Just think how much time and agony went into your own development as a seller. Unless you are lucky to get people who are even faster learners than you are, you can figure on providing more training for your staff.

Ever hear of Murphy's Law? "Whatever can go wrong, will." Well, Murphy just loves chains of command. It is so easy to assume that new people have enough training. They tell you that they did similar work before. This is where you must ask a few questions.

Some middle managers refuse or sort of "forget" to train newcomers because they fear that a trainee might leapfrog over them to a better job. This is one of the reasons my type of training course is in such demand. I won't allow leapfrogging in the classroom, but I don't care what my students do during recess.

Go back and look at your three *i*'s, If you do a good job on the first *i*, the other two should be a lot easier to achieve. Part of our inspirational efforts will be included in your instructive program. Explaining the why and wherefore of your insistence makes a very instructive talk.

In your teaching you will do well to remember your own reaction to speakers who have dumped too much information on you all at once. It took you years to gather your information and know-how. You do not have to stretch out the educational process that long, but it is better to keep your lessons short. It is better to have your student wishing for more information than praying that you sprain your throat.

Keep your temper. A bit of impatient sarcasm will live

in your student's memory long after the points of the lesson are forgotten.

Use understandable language. Too many instructors like to "hot-dog" it with fancy words. They succeed only in demonstrating their vocabularies and their stuffed egos. Simple words that describe the essentials will do the trick. Your students will soon see that their tasks can be completed. Your employees will also appreciate the fact that your instructions are helping get the job done.

Training Never Ends

Your organization must be geared to continual education. Training and retraining will always be necessary. Just think about the computer revolution. Ten years ago only the corporate giants had computers. Now children play with them in the family room. If you add a computer to your operation, your people will need to learn how to use it.

Many say, and I agree, that the average worker today should be retrained about four times in a lifetime. Sometimes new training is necessary to gain greater versatility in your workers. The more "hats" your people wear, the more ways they can help: in the warehouse, on the retail floor, ordering, in the field, wherever needed. You are in special need of "switch hitters" during vacation time, to meet seasonal demands, and when others are out sick.

There are a number of new, aggressive airlines such as People Express which expect everyone to do almost everything. They do not expect baggage handlers to pilot the planes, but pilots can be called on to carry the luggage. The president of the company has even stowed a few bags. (Not only that, he even got them on the right planes!)

Getting the Work Done: Supervising

To get first-class performance from your employees, you have to provide top-grade leadership. I find that good work-

ers all over the country respond to firm, confident leadership. Employees want strong, well-grounded supervisors
who manifest five essential traits:

1. *Frankness*. State what must be done. There is no
coddling of drones.

2. *Sincerity*. (Did you hear the country store cynic's
definition of insincerity? "An undertaker who looks sad at a
$10,000 funeral.")

3. *Tact*. You must know the "on" from the "off" switch.
Your job is to turn people on, not off.

4. *Integrity*. When you are always honest you do not
have to strain your brain remembering what you said. Your
employee will not have to weight your words, because she
knows you have already weighed them and found them not
wanting in truth. To safeguard your credibility do not
hesitate to eat your share of the crow when you turn out to
be wrong. Surely your people will be fair enough to recognize the difference between mistake and a lie. Should you,
the saints forbid, actually tell a lie, admit that too. Get it off
your chest, and start over. There are those who think
Watergate would have been forgotten as quickly as a campaign promise if the president had simply said, "I goofed."

5. *Fairness*. This will win you respect if it does nothing
else. Even an employee who dislikes you can respect you if
you treat everyone fairly.

No business should operate without the "Basic Big
Five." Yet more is needed. In our great nation we have a
sturdy backbone—the Constitution—yet our lawmakers
must continually build on this strong framework with new
laws and changes in old statutes. As lawmaker for your
company I suggest you ponder these eight "statutes." You
may need others, but these at least will steer you in the
right direction:

1. Set objectives for your employees, how much you
expect them to produce. You know what you need for rent,
salary, commissions, upkeep, raw materials, utilities, dividends, interest payments, and something for yourself and
your family. The figure you arrive at is your monthly goal:

$50,000, $100,000, whatever. Your quarterly and semian-nual goals may be correspondingly higher to accent the idea of intended growth.

Now break your overall goal down into units or dollar amounts each person needs to sell; that's their individual goal. To sweeten the pot you might set up incentives: a copy of *Becoming a Superstar Seller* to all who make the quar-terly goal and a trip to their favorite fishing lodge for the best six-month record.

2. Have a detailed plan for obtaining your objectives. You might set up a prospect-finding search as part of your first month's plan. For each month of the half-year segment you might highlight something special: new products, spe-cial prices, or group plans. Give some channels into which the goal-induced enthusiasm can flow.

3. Get daily or weekly progress reports. Otherwise the fires you lit with your original plan will go out. Dieters, investors, spectators, politicians—everyone likes to know how things are going. It helps to spur the laggers and give the leaders their second wind.

4. Always be conscious of the value of individual atten-tion. You can reach more people at a general meeting, but you can better serve the diverse needs and capabilities of your people by one-on-one contacts.

5. Expect excellence. "Good enough is not good enough." You will win respect as a leader by demanding good work. About the only second-rate effort you can tolerate is an employee who is slow to respond to the quitting-time whis-tle.

6. Give recognition for superior effort. Sometimes—oftener than you think—it is the hope of being noticed that prompts workers to rise above the general level. When your hands get callouses from patting backs you can switch to smiles.

7. Follow-up is important. When an assignment has been made, allow enough time for reasonable progress, then make a friendly check. If you wait too long your

employee will think you are not interested. Worse yet, you may forget about the whole thing yourself.

8. The leader should lead. Employees expect the boss to be different, to have a touch of class in thinking, speaking, dressing, enduring, patience, imagination, courtesy—anything that characterizes ladies and gentlemen.

Motivation Begins with You

There is an old baseball maxim: "A manager is not better than his players." If the team is sinking toward the cellar, the baseball manager has two choices: get better players or improve the ones he already has on the team.

Theoretically, a business manager has the same two choices. In practice, though, it's usually a better idea to try to improve the "players" you have through training and motivation. Your people are the result of your best recruiting efforts and are likely to be as good as or better than the results of any second attempt. Besides, your second recruiting attempt may be just picking from the leftovers of the first try.

If your company is like most, you'll have many different types of people working for you. Your job is to get your diverse elements together to get the best out of them—and out of yourself. You must convince them that most of their goals are the same as yours. The specifics may be different. Some may have kids to put through medical school. Some want to buy a resort condominium. You may want to endow a youth club. But there are some things you all have in common. You want the basics. You want respect, and freedom from unnecessary fears. You want recognition for your efforts, both financial and intangible. You want a hearing for your ideas. You want to trust and be trusted.

To motivate your workers you need an open-door policy. An open-purse policy helps, but that's only part of it. In my own experience, hard-to-approach bosses were actually demotivators. All of them gave me raises, but none of them made me happy to work for them.

The Minnesota Vikings are good examples of what I mean. They are not as flashy as some fans might like, but they have been in three Super Bowls and most of the playoffs. Their salaries are not the greatest, but players usually stay on the roster as long as they can. They know they will be treated with consistency. Win, lose, or draw, people in the Viking organization are treated with respect and consideration.

Every winning sports organization has that extra spark that enthusiasm gives. Surely you have read of teams that were loaded with talent but were defeated by outfits with poorer records. The losing coach will usually offer just one basic excuse: "The boys were flat. They just were not up for the game—no enthusiasm."

You can have a roster of masters of business administration but still fail if they are half-hearted in their approach to the job at hand. Your motivation should do more than just bring your people to work on time and keep them awake while they're there. If you can only inspire your people to go through the motions, you're going to stand still—at best.

You have to build enthusiasm. You have to get the kind of spirit that will prompt a clerk to remain in your store to serve a customer who walks in at quitting time. You need the kind of enthusiasm that will breed ideas for better display, better products, and better selling methods. You should want to have an epidemic of broken sales records, greater production, and innovative promotional ideas. Fortunately, enthusiasm can be contagious. And it starts with you.

Incidentally, everything I've said about motivating and managing people still applies if you're only managing yourself. Self-management is often the toughest job of all. Too often the person trying to manage herself or himself must work on someone who is conceited, ill-informed, lazy, short-tempered, impatient, slovenly, opinionated, prejudiced, irreligious, and short of breath.

The Manager's First Commandment: Employees Are Human Beings

Public relations should start with the public closest to you: your people. As a manager, you must be able to distinguish between your merchants and your merchandise. Your merchandise is a thing—good, bad, or indifferent. Your merchants are people; they can laugh or cry, sing or moan, feel great or hurt like hell, be honest or steal you blind, grow or decay. How they perform has a lot to do with you. Your attitude will show up in the warmth of your smile, the sincerity of your handshake, your willingness to listen, and your concern for your people.

Unless you are in charge of IBM, I would suggest you sit down with each employee and have a private talk. Your chat should cover your mutual goals, what your employee expects of you, and what you expect of her or him. I like to give an encouraging word: "If you work with me, and I work with you, you are going to see that we can both make music. We are both going to get what we want out of this business."

It takes times to do this, but consider how much time you spend with cronies. Are they putting the meat on your table, or is it the office boy who idolizes you and would give his rock and roll records for a chance to visit with you? Are the players in your golf or bridge foursome helping you declare a dividend, or is it the charwoman who gets down on her hands and knees to make your office presentable? Sure, spend time with your friends; you earned it. But don't shortchange your employees. *They* earned it. If they haven't earned a bit of your time by now, what are you keeping them for?

For five and a half years I was the number-one producer for a certain company. One morning I cornered the manager. "George, I've been here over five years, so just for the heck of it, what's my wife's name?" He couldn't even think of "Mrs."

I tried again. "I've had three children since I came here." I doubt if he even knew I was married. Right then and there I quit. The boss only thought about me in terms of my million dollars in sales.

I worked for another company for a solid ten years, day and night, six days a week, and numerous weekends. Yet I had to wait 90 days to get an appointment with the head of the company. I figured I had reached the end of the line, and got off the bus.

I would have stayed with either company. Their products were good; the pay was fine; my territories were gold mines. Everything was fine except the most important thing: concern about me. Other companies have lost their real breadwinners for similar reasons. You can easily avoid such a silly mistake by a small dose of decency and concern.

To keep abreast of your employees you could easily compile a looseleaf book about them. Give each person a page with a small picture. The first entry might be the date he or she started. Subsequent entries might contain a wide range of information about their job achievements and their personal milestones. You might have to add another page when you start adding pictures of grandchildren. Use the book to refresh your memory, and use the information as often as you can.

This kind of personal touch will go a long way toward building stability in your company. Stability is enhanced by the number of "lifers" in your employ. They are people who stay with you year after year, people who do not have to be handled as raw recruits. They may need training to keep up with our changing world, but they know your system.

And when it comes time for your "lifer" to retire, at the retirement party you could present a bound copy of the memory book. It won't cost much more than the traditional watch that primarily reminds retirees they're over the hill.

Supervising Is Something You Do Every Day

Generally speaking, in any group of 100, you will find 2 who are motivated enough to be self-starters, 23 who need supervision to maintain their momentum, and 75 who cannot function without a boss. Very few people can put it all together; most salespeople need supervision.

Good supervision determines your company's profits. Give your selling staff clear-cut directions about what they can do and how they should do it. If they want to know why, you can tell them, "So you and your family can eat." As a silent prayer you might add, "And mine too."

Supervisors of any worker—even the one-task type—must engage in almost continuous, day-to-day coaching. You must be alert every working hour to appraise the work done, to show how it should be accomplished, or to encourage workers who find certain tasks difficult or confusing.

I'm going to repeat myself because that's what you must do. You must constantly monitor your people. Get reports. Check what they do. Do not assume a thing.

You may have to encourage workers at certain onerous chores like hauling, pushing, pulling, polishing, sweeping, and listening to complaints. There is no fun in these tasks, so at least give their handlers the enjoyment of your praise and good wishes.

Modern management requires leadership rather than drivership. Snapping whips is for herds. (Keep in mind that management and leadership are not necessarily found in the same person. You may do better in the background, directing the person who leads for you.)

You may find that your really good salespeople are likely to be mavericks, but wouldn't you rather have a spirited horse that can really run than a docile old cart horse? It takes a good rider to set a powerful, strong-willed stallion, but that combination does most of the work on a ranch. The same is true of a manager who can harness the explosive energy of fellow superstars.

Being a Good Boss

Be ready to give a hand with problems. I remember with extreme distaste a boss who left me to work overtime while he went golfing. Before long, I left him.

When people make suggestions, show interest. Take time to hear out the idea. At least suggest a detailed write-up of the plan. Employees show they care when they try to be helpful. You must exercise patience. None of your workers has the stake in the business that you have. If you give them a bigger piece of the pie with a profit-sharing plan, you can demand more. Otherwise, you cannot expect the same devotion as you show for your enterprise.

When employees walk the extra mile, make a fuss over them. Trips, gold plaques, lunches, even a friendly handshake, are all ways you tell good employees "there is more where that came from."

Reward good performance. The minimum wage is fair, but people who exceed the minimum amount of work should be paid more. The minimum would be showing up on time, telling the truth most of the time, making enough sales to cover expenses. So anyone who comes early to arrange stock, always tells the truth, and sells enough to make a profit should make more money.

When someone complains about Jane Doe's raise, you have a golden opportunity. Tell the complainer, "I'm glad you asked. Now, I think you should be getting a raise too, but this is what you have to do first. . . ."

I have always made it my policy to grant a small raise when my employees increased their output, demonstrated their cooperation, or improved their attitude. In every case, I gave the raise without being asked. A surprise raise, even a small one, can work wonders. Try it sometime.

Say you gave an employee a surprise raise of one percent, $1 for every $100. Do you think you'd get a one percent increase in effort? I can't say for sure, but I'll guess you'd get at least that. Would it be worth the extra $1? A New York accounting firm states that a one percent increase in your employees' efforts can bring you a seven percent growth in profits. This is a concrete, dollars-and-cents example of what I mean by first class. The difference of one percent in effort yields a seven percent margin of profit. That's a dollar well spent.

Correct with Care

When you need to correct an employee, use the human relations sandwich. Start with praise at the bottom, add the criticism, then top it off with another slice of praise. The criticism will taste like boarding-house steak, but if the praise is tasty the whole thing will be easier to swallow.

For example, Bill is a good worker but has been late several times. So tell him, "Bill, you have done a good job for us, but you have been late several times. People like you are too necessary. We don't like to try to get along without you even for a short time.

Here's another example: "Lil, you have just the personality to sell the Throckmorton estate, but dole out your charm more evenly. Mrs. Throckmorton is madder than a wet hen. She just called and ranted on and on that you were flirting with her husband. I wouldn't be telling you this, but I know you can dry the feathers of a wet hen—but don't tell her I said that."

Never correct anyone in a crowd. Praise is also better saved for private opportunities. In a group, praise of one person could be construed as left-handed criticism of the others present. You could easily get nine people sore at you because you praised the tenth.

Correcting faults is part of the instructive task of a manager. In some cases it may be the toughest job you will face as a manager: correcting the mistake you made when you hired the error-prone person. Sometimes firing is the only way you can correct a fault.

Do not feel sorry for yourself. Just go ahead and do it. You are not doing a square peg a favor by driving it into a round hole. No one likes to discharge an employee, but by failing to eliminate nonproductive people you could bring down your entire house of cards.

The Sweet Smell of Success

When your employees succeed, you succeed. Remember this, and don't make the mistake of becoming envious of anyone who takes over and actually does better at a task than you did. This just means that you are a better manager than you thought.

Anyone who feels threatened by aggressive young recruits has no business being in management. Your job is to get out the work, to make profits, and to build a strong, lasting organization. If your staff makes more in commissions than you do, count your blessings. You are making more than you would without them.

Some may object: "But that's not fair that a salesperson should get more than the owner of the business." Forget it. Life is not fair.

There are compensations. When the president of the United States attends a Redskins game in RFK Stadium he may be applauding people who make more than he does. He is, nevertheless, the president.

CHAPTER 13

Loyalty Is a Many-Faceted Asset

Attitude is like a chowder: tasty and nourishing, or blah and even harmful. It depends on the cook. If he uses good basic ingredients and seasons it with the right spices, his guests become boosters. If he uses freezer-burned fish plus the wrong spices, his victims may nibble the crackers, but they will barely sip the soup, particularly if it is only warm.

The attitude of a seller is, of course, made up of many intangibles, including some basics and some embellishments. For attitude to be good, there must be more than a dash of loyalty. To have it any other way would be to confuse the food with the spice. Loyalty is as basic to good attitude as fresh seafood is to good chowder. You can go even further and say that it is as basic as heat. Loyalty has to be strong enough—or if you prefer, hot enough—to warm us when we ourselves are cold.

You find "hot loyalty" in all sorts of persons, places, and situations. Oddly enough, fervid allegiance often exists where it doesn't matter. The dogged devotion of Brooklyn fans for the Dodgers ball club—"dem bums"—was legendary. Now the team is based in Los Angeles, but life goes on in Brooklyn. As long as there's a comedian on the East Coast, there will always be a Brooklyn.

It is possible to sell without real loyalty, especially when someone else has opened up the market, or when the product or service is in short supply, or when the seller is on an expense account plus a draw. The mediocre seller needs no loyalty.

But a superstar seller has many loyalties that make him or her do a better job. Men and women who rise anywhere near the top are loyal to several or all of the following: themselves, their parents, their God, their country, their families, their bosses, their employees, their friends, their bird dogs (those good folks who send business your way), their churches, their clubs, and, in a very special way, their customers.

Loyalty to Yourself

Far too many people in all walks of life are really their own most relentless enemies. Usually they act as though they have no loyalty *other* than to themselves. But don't be mistaken about the true nature of self-pampering. It is, so to speak, killing oneself with kindness.

Joe bought out a good restaurant that was going in high gear. If anything requires a lot of selling, it is a café. With everyone who can open a can of soup deciding to become an eatery operator, Joe found himself competing with numerous places, which he sometimes frequented almost as much as his own. Maybe he was just "scouting the enemy," but buying rounds for admirers at other bars put an extra strain on the overhead at his own emporium.

Worst of all, Joe became more and more of a night person. When he should have been in his office to do the things he couldn't do during service hours, Joe was catching up on lost sleep. So his receipts got smaller and smaller as the bills became larger and larger. Before long, he was forced to unload his business.

Joe's story is repeated over and over in many different ways: the dress shop operator who plays the grand lady instead of doing with less help, the peddler who has to stop for a quick one before his first call (and at too late an hour), the charmer who flirts with a customer, or the contractor who uses the company crew to build his new garage, house, or lake cottage.

This last item reminds me of a printer who had agreed to have a special and much-needed order ready for me by Saturday noon. It was so important that I drove down to the shop to check on the progress. I was told by a janitor that "the boys are helping Bud with his new swimming pool." I hit the ceiling, the panic button, and high C with my yell of outrage.

Good old Bud almost lost $500 in monthly billings because he wasn't loyal enough to his own interests to postpone his fancy project until he could afford to. Having the first outdoor swimming tank in town is one thing. Losing a business—which Bud actually did later on—is another.

Loyalty to Your Country

Don't forget about your country—our country. Can you put everything you make into your pocket? Far too many try. A growing number of million-dollar incomes get by scot free. An untold amount of cash income is undeclared. Often the effort at concealment of income is more ingenious than the strategies to acquire it. I am not talking about the French or Colombian connections or about the Cosa Nostra. I am talking about Mr. Good Guy.

This is not superstar selling, or business, or management, or super anything. Apart from the ethics of out-and-out tax avoidance, it is also stupid. Should you ever choose to sell your business you will have to show your track record. You will not be very convincing telling your buyer: "You understand, of course, nowadays you deal in cash. You can figure another seventy percent added onto what shows on these books."

Your buyer may buy that, but if she does she is not going to be smart enough to run the business and pay you too. Most likely your explanation will cause her to wonder, "If the seller is shoving it to the government, how about me?"

But do we have to gauge our commercial practices on the basis of so-called hard-nosed practicality? I think not. Remember, we are not setting up super money machines, but super people. According to a recent study the most profitable enterprise in this country is organized crime: drugs, illegal gambling, extortion, and theft. The practitioners of these arts pay no taxes on their basic incomes. The underground untaxed economy, according to government estimate, is $222 billion.

In 1981 there were 304 Americans who declared $200,000 incomes or more yet paid no federal income tax. I may be a super "square," but to me, it appears that there are far too many freeloaders in our country. They have the loyalty of the proverbial dog that bites the hand that feeds it.

Wealthy people? Undoubtedly. Superstars? Not a chance.

Loyalty to Your Family

With 50 percent of all marriages going on the rocks it is obvious that modern family loyalty is much too thin. Each person has to decide this matter. You may decide it is too much of a demand on your resources to be loyal to your spouse and children. This is your prerogative, but be prepared to pay the price. I know hundreds of people who choose this self-oriented route. I would not change places with any of them.

When you choose to play fair with your family, you give yourself another support in your pursuit of superstardom: good motivation. You are motivated to save for the education of your children and for better living in general. You are inspired to avoid the traps that wreck careers as well as marriages: drinking, drugs, casual flirtations, and general self-indulgence.

Loyalty to Your Boss

Loyalty to the boss is not a common virtue. To put it another way, disloyalty is commonplace. One of the most disloyal employees I ever encountered was one to whom I gave a chance after she had lost a similar job because of her intoxication at a luncheon meeting. I was desperate; I had to stay away from my high-tension job for at least two months. I returned after my absence to find my staff, with one exception, completely intractable. I think I would rather have an employee who got drunk on the job than one who undercut my authority and credibility.

Loyalty to Your Staff

As much as we sometimes would like to choke employees, we have to be loyal to them, even when they are disloyal to us. The lady I just mentioned was even the beneficiary of my personal sacrifice. Because of her family obligations I cut my own draw from the business to add to her salary. I would do it again for an employee.

Your people make a positive contribution to your well-being. Your good helpers, even the slowpokes, are not mere numbers. They have the same basic wants, needs, and yearnings as you do. They deserve a decent share in the good things they help you generate through your company: decent wages, recognition, enjoyment, a sense of security, and a feeling of accomplishment.

Loyalty to Your Customers

Finally, I am going to jump to the customers, people who deserve a very special loyalty. They make your enterprise possible.

I know people who hardly recognize their customers. Fair-weather friends too often win the comradeship that should go to good customers. Who, after all, is the better friend—the people who accept your hospitality or the people who make it possible?

CHAPTER 14

Profile
of a
Superstar Seller

Almost everyone would agree with me that "There aren't many superstars, but everybody wants to be one." Maybe we can't all agree on what makes a superstar, but some things will be the same in everyone's description.

Superstars are likely to be self-contained, like the bedrock on which engineers like to build. They have no need to maintain their egos. They are not threatened by competition, spurred to more action, maybe, but not threatened, especially not by weaklings.

I often think of a St. Bernard I once saw. A small chihuahua was skipping around the large dog, incessantly and insistently yelping. For about five minutes the massive dog endured the half-pint's scolding. Finally, the tormentor moved in too close. With no change in its sad, long-suffering expression, the huge dog majestically raised a front paw and laid it gently on the back of the canine termite, which collapsed like a Chippendale chair under the weight of a sumo wrestler.

In summary, here are some things we know about superstar sellers. They usually:

Dress and act differently.
Work long and late.
Are better organized.
Are willing to work two to ten years to put an item over.
Act like wild ducks out of Canada.
Think differently.
Are typically loners.
Are nocturnal.
Have "hyper" personalities.
Are avid readers of self-help books.
Are dreamers.
Are most likely to be hired.
Bring in more money than anyone else in a five-year period.
Do great research.
Spend more time in preparation.
Love to experiment.
Are willing to stay up nights writing up a deal.
Will spend two or three nights per week preparing.
Are willing to work one to three extra hours per day.
Are information gatherers.
Know how to size up people.
Are adept at using their own judgment.
Occasionally break down emotionally.

Become frustrated and anxious.
Win and win.
Are known as champions, leaders, and
 pacesetters.
Talk differently.
Talk about tomorrow.
Never mention yesterday.
Can fire up a whole campaign.
Try different approaches.
Always use their imaginations.
Look at things differently.
Are natural leaders.
Always want to be in charge of their
 group.
Will work night and day to exceed
 quotas.
Work for big and small companies.
Can sell four to five times more than the
 average.
Are a different breed of people.
Are the "firecrackers" that move a
 company ahead.
Excel as workers.
Keep bottom lines in the black.
Are committed, dedicated people.
Make the difference between profit and
 loss.
Sometimes seem obnoxious.
Are impatient with others.
Can be cranky and irritable.
May seem egotistical.
Will work from 6 A.M. to 9 P.M. with no
 ill effects.
Outthink and outsell just to beat others.
Can double the profits of a company in a
 two-year period.
Are fast learners.
Can put it all together quickly.

Love other people's ideas.
Need to be "stroked" often.
Are not often administrative types.
Have a great belief in themselves.
Become obsessed with ideas.
Are workaholics. ✓
Work night and day making sales calls. ✓
Are fanatics—like Edison.
Always look for better ideas.
Explode the fetters that tie up the clods.
Are often promoted to the top.
Love to "throw touchdown passes."
Are restless if they don't have an order.
Are totally committed to their jobs.
Willingly endure trial by fire and live
*   with uncertainty.*
Can save a company.

In short, superstars are not like the brief explosion of giant skyrockets. They are permanent lights in the panorama of the upper regions. They are the celestial lights by which the venturesome can travel the lonely road to glory.

★★★★★★★★★★★ Index ★★★★★★★★★★★★